SELF-HYPNOSIS
The Key to Athletic Success

John G. Kappas, Ph.D., has more than thirty years' professional experience in hypnotherapy, sex therapy, and relationship counseling. In his efforts to upgrade the practice and public opinion of hypnosis and hypnotherapy, Dr. Kappas founded the American Hypnosis Association in 1968 and the Hypnotist's Union, AFL-CIO, in 1973. He is responsible for taking hypnosis out of the entertainment field by creating a federal Dictionary of Occupational Titles definition for hypnotherapy, thereby establishing it as a viable therapeutic intervention. He is the author of several other psychology books, most recently *Improve Your Sex Life Through Self-Hypnosis* (PANORAMA PUBLISHING COMPANY).

JOHN G. KAPPAS, Ph.D.

SELF-HYPNOSIS
THE KEY TO ATHLETIC SUCCESS

PANORAMA
PUBLISHING
COMPANY

18607 Ventura Boulevard, Suite 310, Tarzana, CA 91356

Library of Congress Cataloging in Publication Data

Kappas, John G.
  Self-hypnosis—the key to athletic success.

  Includes index.
    1. Sports—Psychological aspects.   2. Autogenetic
training.   I. Title.
GV706.4.K37 1984   796'.01   84-11617
ISBN 0-13-803321-8
ISBN 0-13-803313-7 (pbk.)

1 2 3 4 5 6 7 8 9 10

ISBN 0-13-803321-8

ISBN 0-13-803313-7 {PBK.}

Cover design by Hal Siegel
Manufacturing buyer: Pat Mahoney

Contents

SELF-HYPNOSIS
The Key to Athletic Success

Self-hypnosis:
the key to
athletic success

1

"She won the race before it began!" said the incredulous sports announcer. He had just witnessed the finest women athletes from around the world compete in a grueling 1500-meter run. Yet there was one woman who led from the start, dominating the race despite the fact that previously she had always lost when in competition with the same quality runners.

No one had cheated; no one tried to perform at less than her best effort. There was just something about the winner's attitude, an attitude evident from the moment she stepped to the starting block, that seemed to indicate she knew she would win. It was an aura of triumph that appeared to dominate and restrain the other runners, keeping them from ever truly being able to challenge her lead.

"She won the race before it began." How many times have you heard some variation of that phrase in athletic competition? Sometimes it refers to a boxer whose very presence in the ring tells you that he will triumph that day, regardless of the skill or reputation of his opponent. Or it might be heard on the golf course where one player, perhaps a typical "duffer" in the past, has played the best eighteen holes of his life.

The triumph might happen in the bowling alley or on the football field. It might occur on the tennis court or while playing racquetball, soccer, basketball, baseball, or any other sport. It can happen with an individual player or with the entire team. However it occurs, there seems to be some electrically charged magnetism about the player, amateur or professional, and you know he or she is going to have what may be the finest performance to date.

The reality of sports, any sport, is that at any given time none of the competitors is likely to be performing at anything near peak ability. All of us are capable of seven to nine times more strength and endurance than we normally achieve. This great reserve of strength can be observed when a ninety-pound woman suddenly lifts a 2000-pound car when it accidentally rolls on her child. Not only is the woman unhurt by the feat; she is amazed that she even attempted such an "impossible" act. Yet the power forced upon her by the terror of the moment could, with training, be deliberately tapped for voluntary use in athletic competition.

The purpose of this book is to help you achieve your greatest potential as an amateur or professional athlete. It does not matter if you are a senior citizen whose golf score has yet to come anywhere near your age or a teenager hoping to succeed on the college football team. You might be an avid tennis player, a weekly bowler, a body builder, a baseball player, or anything else. You might be male or female, young or old, physically handicapped or in the prime of your health. Whatever the case, you are going to learn the secret of tapping that inner ability which results in achievements beyond your previous greatest expectations.

What Is Self-Hypnosis?

Self-hypnosis is nothing more than the way you learn to focus your mind on a particular task or idea. It is a tool for personal achievement as important as the natural build of your body, the state of your health, and your personal conditioning program. It is a method for influencing your performance which can help you to win or insure that you fail.

For example, have you ever seen a boxing match between two top heavyweight fighters? Both men are in peak condition. Both have been spending weeks sparring with excellent boxers, studying films of their opponents' fighting styles, running several miles a day for stamina, and otherwise building their bodies to perfection. They have also been involved in shouting matches and publicity stunts in which each talks about the horrible violence and mayhem which will be visited upon the head of the opponent.

Then comes the day of the fight. By all standards of age, size, and physical conditioning, the two men are perfectly matched. Each is a skilled fighter with an enviable win-loss record. Either man should be able to win the fight that day, except for an unspoken difference. One of the opponents, and sometimes both contenders, has been reading all the stories in the newspaper about the potential outcome of the fight. The boxer has seen the odds determined by the sports-writers and the gamblers. He has learned all the reasons why his oppo-nent is the "certain" victor and why he will be lucky to go the distance. And, for some reason, this prefight publicity has taken its toll. You can tell that no matter how much this man thinks he is going to give his all, he is actually going to fail. He has let himself be convinced he will lose, and the only thing that will save him is if his opponent has come to the same personal conclusion and is also at less than psychological perfection. The victory in the ring is ultimately determined not just by the training but also by the subconscious beliefs of each fighter.

Or take a different sport, competitive swimming. Again, each swimmer has been in training for many weeks. Each has developed his or her body to perfection. Yet each person enters the meet with an awareness of the crowd's favorite. This favorite might belong to a swim club whose members are known to frequently emerge victorious because of superior training. Or it might be someone whose past triumphs make this person the swimmer to be beaten. Whatever the case, all the contenders sense the "reality" and seem to adjust their performances accordingly. They think they are placing their maximum effort into the meet, yet they are actually likely to hold back slightly because they "know" they can not beat the favorite.

Then a "miracle" happens. One of the swimmers, someone who has decided that she cannot win that day yet is not going to be dis-couraged from doing her best, suddenly realizes she is in the lead. The crowd favorite, the person she expected to dominate the meet, is several lengths behind. At that instant, her mind suddenly explodes with the reality that she is a winner. She realizes that if she just maintains the pace which has brought her so comfortably to this commanding position, she actually will win the race. Suddenly nothing will stop her, including a last-minute burst of speed by her rival, and she takes control of the race, the "dark horse" swimming to victory.

You have seen this same effect happen with whatever sport you enjoy. The outcome is decided as much by the mental attitude of the competitors as it is by the quality of their preparation. The bowler with a fifty-pin handicap "feels lucky" and proceeds to bowl an almost perfect game for the first time in his life. The tennis player tires of ridicule from the club champ and suddenly finds that every ball he or she sends is placed perfectly, in bounds yet just out of reach of the opponent. The long-distance runner who has never gone the distance suddenly finds that the pace is easier, not only finishing but actually coming across the line ahead of many of the other competitors. Whatever the circumstances, and they can be as varied as the number of sporting events, the difference in performance is the result of the tapping of the subconscious mind. It is the sudden inner awareness that you can succeed which results in your personal triumph. And the key to this awareness is self-hypnosis.

Self-hypnosis is not a shortcut to success. You cannot sit on a couch, drinking beer, never exercising, watching old fight films of the triumphs of Muhammad Ali, and expect to have self-hypnosis change you into a heavyweight championship contender. You will always have to learn the rules of the game you want to play, practice the techniques involved in the sport, and develop your body to the best of your ability for the competition. Self-hypnosis is not an alternative to running long distances if you want to triumph in the Boston Marathon, for example. Yet once you have taken the trouble to learn the sport and develop your body, you can use self-hypnosis to give you that winning edge.

Is Self-Hypnosis "Cheating"?

The reality of athletics is that every great champion, regardless of field, uses self-hypnosis to win. The person may not always realize that this is what he or she is doing. Sometimes the person refers to precompetition meditation or the mental reviewing of the game about to be played. At other times the athlete may use the term "psyching up" for the match. At still other times the person may say that he or she simply is planning to keep the opponent "constantly off guard." Yet each term refers to the same action, the use of self-hypnosis to achieve peak ability.

The problem for most athletes is that this mental process is not so well planned as it should be. They have not learned how to effectively use self-hypnosis on a regular basis, and many, such as boxers reading the prefight publicity, may use it negatively against themselves. Thus, while self-hypnosis is certainly a proper tool for success in athletics, it is often misunderstood, underused, and improperly used.

What You Are Going to Learn from This Book

This book is going to teach you not only self-hypnosis for any sport you enjoy, but maximum potential every time you enjoy athletics. It does not matter whether you are young or old, male or female, amateur or professional, handicapped or in perfect health. Each sport will be discussed in a separate chapter, and you will be taught how to use self-hypnosis for maximum achievement. There will also be a section for the physically handicapped who are enjoying athletics, often as part of a rehabilitation or health-maintenance program, so that you can use self-hypnosis to safely improve your achievements.

The methods you will learn have been developed and tested with thousands of amateur and professional athletes throughout the country. I am a hypnotherapist with a great love of sports as well as someone who had to learn to strengthen his own performance after experiencing serious physical illness. I have helped aging amateurs and individuals whose names read like a *Who's Who* of both international competition and professional teams throughout the United States. I know the information you are about to receive will work for you just as it has proven successful for so many others.

Now turn to the next chapter to begin learning how you can apply the secrets of self-hypnosis to your athletic goals. Although the bulk of the chapters are devoted to individual sports, you may want to read every chapter, not just the ones which relate to the activities you most enjoy. You will find that the methods so successful for others may be adaptable to your interests as well. But no matter how you use this book, you will find that you will begin achieving success beyond your greatest expectations.

Why you're having problems learning a sport

2

Sports are difficult to learn. Everyone knows that. Take golf, for example. You have this little ball and all those clubs. You've got to figure out how to hit the ball toward a green you can barely see and get it into a tiny hole that is invisible when you tee off.

Or take tennis. What a deceptive sport that is! You've got this racket and the net, and supposedly all you have to do is hit the ball where your opponent isn't and you win the point. But look at the reality of the game. All these stores sell these special rackets with different woods and metals, different stringings, different configurations for the design. . . . And the professionals; they earn hundreds of thousands of dollars at the very least. Nobody pays that kind of money if the game isn't impossible for anyone but a genius to master, right?

Or take bowling. You've got this ball with holes and all those pins to knock over. Looks pretty simple, so why do they have the lines, the gutter, the wrist protector, the weight evaluator for the ball, the special shoes, the teaching pros, and all the money paid to the men and women who bowl on television? You got it. It's a rough game.

Even running. You can't go out and run and expect to do anything but get winded, right? If running was so easy, why would there be sixteen brands of shoes, Gatorade®, the special clothing, the chronometer, 143 different books, and terms like "hitting the wall"? I don't know about you, but I become exhausted just thinking about the seemingly impossible task of running around the block. The marathons? The mini-marathons? The "fun runs" for charity? That's for the professional, not for you and me. Right?

The Myth of Sports

There is a great myth about athletics, a myth which is much like what you have just read. No matter what the sport, whether you are part of a team or playing individually, you are constantly reminded of how poor a player you are.

Take the image of sports projected by television, for example. If you knew just how easy it was to achieve maximum performance in any sport you enjoy, would you bother watching it on television? Possibly and possibly not. Most certainly you would not hold the athletes in great awe. You would not go out and buy the clothing and equipment they endorse. You would not tolerate the antics of some of the players when they stomp around the playing fields, cursing the officials, making obscene gestures to the grandstand audience, and demanding champagne in their hotel bathtubs. You would simply consider them spoiled brats in adult bodies, not "super stars" whose genius at the game allows them to have special privileges.

Then there are the equipment manufacturers. They have a stake in maintaining the myth of athletics. If you thought that even the simplest equipment would enable you to compete with the pros, you would not buy the $75 shoes, the $150 rackets, the designer clothing emblazoned with the magic name of an athlete that allows you to spend 35 percent more (the fee for the use of that name) than that same clothing would cost without the special feature. You would not be constantly changing brands, adding special gadgets, believing in the magic amulets of the newest wrist straps, headbands, and other devices.

Finally, there are the numerous businesses unrelated to the sports field, such as office supply houses, rental car agencies, restaurants, and hotels. They use Arnie, and Chrissie, and Joe, and O.J., and Debbie, and anyone else who is today's favorite. The implication given is that these athletes are gods with powers and abilities far beyond those of mortal humans. If you buy the copier, dictation unit, computer, television set, restaurant special, or whatever else they're selling, you will have that same super power working for you. Now do you think that the advertiser wants you to feel you are as skilled as your favorite professional? I'm not going to buy the copier John Kappas recommends because I know that I don't know as much about copiers as the man who won the Boston Marathon or the woman who beat Billie Jean or Chrissie or Evonne six sets to nothing. They're the real copier experts, right?

Do I sound facetious? Do I seem to be less than reverent about the greats of the sporting world? More importantly, am I making you a little uncomfortable by demythologizing some of the great American sales efforts? Good, that's what I want to do.

The truth is that you might be a far better athlete in whatever sport you either enjoy or are now trying to learn than all the greats you have idolized. This does not mean that you can play golf with the U.S. Open Champion and expect to beat him (though it is possible). It does not mean that you could enter the Wimbledon Tennis Tournament and emerge triumphant, though every year a newcomer has that chance. Nor does it mean that you are going to break the three-minute mile or run twenty-six miles faster than your competition, though again there is the possibility. What it does mean is that you can improve your abilities to the point where you are equal to your present potential, then begin improving even beyond that level. And when you do, you may be more skilled for the time in which you are involved than the greats you see as your idols.

The Myth of the Professional

Most professional athletes have a very narrow focus of interest and ability. Usually from the time they are very small, one sport is the driving force in their lives. They will work out before school and then after school until well into the night. They eliminate most friendships, except for those with other compulsive participants in their area of interest. They seldom have time to read books, to go to the movies, to socialize, or to lead even a semblance of a normal existence. Their lives are filled with lessons, practice, and thinking about the game. This is true for professionals in tennis, swimming, golf, boxing, karate, track and field, baseball, soccer, and so on through the list of sports.

Take the case of Wendy, a fourth-degree black belt in karate by the time she reached twenty-one. "I began taking lessons when I was thirteen. I was both small for my size and physically well developed," she explained, laughing. "My mother thought that karate would enable me to handle the boys a little easier during puberty. What she didn't realize was how much fun it would be for me.

"I began going after school and staying not just for my class but for every other class until the place closed. If they wouldn't let me work out, I'd watch. I practiced forms before I went to school and worked out during gym class when the teachers would let me. I earned my black belt in less than a year and then began teaching while working towards higher rank.

"I found I would rather do karate than eat or sleep. I began losing weight and being exhausted, but I wouldn't stop training. Finally the owner of the karate school made me get more rest and be a little more sensible than I had been, but I only did it out of respect. I had my own school when I was eighteen and I made fourth degree when I was twenty-one.

"Only now am I beginning to date and do things outside of the karate school. I've begun going to movies, and I'm forcing myself to take an occasional course at the community college in anything that sounds interesting. I feel as though I'm socially still in early adolescence, and I'm desperate to catch up."

Jim, an Olympic swimmer, made similar comments. He started swimming with a club when he was seven. As he improved, he began spending several hours each day in the water. All he thought about was technique and competition. He had few friends outside of the club and spent almost no time on his schoolwork. His grades were extremely poor, and he never could engage in the small talk of kids because he didn't watch much television, read comic books, or have what anyone else would consider a normal childhood. "My whole life was in the pool. It paid off financially. I've made a lot of money doing endorsements and, at twenty-seven, I'm fairly well set for life. But now I've got to find something to do in the real world. I don't want to coach other kids, and I'm not trained for a job. I don't really know what jobs exist out there, and I'm just now starting to find that out."

I have heard the same stories from tennis players, professional golfers, pro bowlers, baseball stars, football stars, boxers, and numerous others. Their profession evolved from an obsession, their skills coming from endless hours of practice.

"But how does this relate to me?" you are probably asking. "All I want to do is improve my skills at basketball [or tennis, or golf, or football, or soccer, or any other athletic interest you might have]. How can you relate me, the total amateur, to one of the professionals?"

It is quite simple. The reason the vast majority of professional athletes are so good is *not* because they have more natural ability than you have. In fact, they may not be so skilled as you are at your current level of play.

The fact is that for the number of hours you have put into learning the sport of interest to you, you might be far superior to the skill level of the athlete you admire when he or she had the same training you have. You are looking at someone with thousands of hours of experience and wondering why you are not as good. The reality is that when the professional had only the experience you have now, he or she might not have been anywhere near as good as you are. You are trying to compare your limited training with someone who has years of experience, and it does not work.

Think about why you have purchased this book. You want to be better than you are, perhaps the best of which you are capable with the time you have to spend on the sport. Chances are that you are not thinking of a career in professional athletics. You are not interested in dropping all other interests in order to become a "super star." You want to hold a job, go to school, have friends, watch television, or do any of the other activities which relate to your circumstances. You do not want to devote your life to mastering a sport so you can earn your living at it. You want to lead a normal existence with the sport being one aspect of your life, not your total focus as is the case with the majority of professional athletes.

In other words, you already may be better than you think you are. If the players around you seem better than you are, it is not because you are bad but because you have not put quite so much time into the activity. You are undoubtedly doing fine where you are, and I am going to show you how to improve faster and more effectively than you ever thought possible. You are going to learn some of the secrets the professionals know but often did not learn until they were well established in their careers. In effect, you will be getting a head start on your idols, developing a mastery of the sport which will always give you satisfaction.

The Myth of Human Limitations

The human body is built in many different sizes and shapes. One person is tall, lean, and long-legged. Another person is squat, with tight muscles and a large-boned frame. Even when two people are the same height, the length of their arms and legs might differ.

Certain bodies make engaging in certain sports much easier. Two runners may move their legs at the same speed, but the runner with the longer stride will win the race. He or she is not faster than the other person. The winner simply has a stride which covers more ground in the same time. Under such circumstances, the loser can either give up ("I'll never be a very good runner because I can't beat Fred or Alice") or practice running faster than in the past. The extra speed will compensate for the opponent's longer stride, turning that "loser" into a winner.

A person who is seven feet tall can be a basketball star with very little skill. The hoop is ten feet from the ground; the player is seven feet tall, with arms that may add another three feet in height. He or she can run to the basket and practically drop the ball through the hoop.

Perhaps you are five feet nine inches tall and you love basketball. You practice lay-ups, jump shots, foul shots, and all the other techniques you know you will need because you will never be able to drop that ball through the hoop. Yet when you go out for your high school or college basketball team, you may have difficulty competing with the extremely tall players because they have such an easy time of the game. Does this mean that they are better than you? No. The reality is that they are not as good.

"But how can this be?" you argue. "The tall players dominate the boards. They can grab the ball from the hoop. They can intimidate me with their size. They never have to try to make a basket from halfway across the court like I do. And there is the reality."

Suppose you raise the basketball hoop to a height proportionately as far from the giants of the game as the ten-feet-high hoop is from you. Now let them try to play because they can no longer just drop the ball through the net. They will have to make the lay-ups and other shots which you have been practicing. Suddenly the "greats" are missing what, for you, would have been easy shots. They have substituted height for skill. You, the beginning player who perhaps works out an hour a day when you have time, suddenly see that you have far more skill than many of the professionals.

The training you receive also seems to glorify the professional athlete. Golf is one of the greatest examples. You are told that you have to keep your head down, your eye on the ball, your wrists carefully placed and locked, your follow-through exactly right, and on and on. You are so busy concentrating on each step of the swing that you forget to relax. You do not think of the end result you are seeking. You think only of how you must handle the swing so that you can be like the professional. As a result, you become tense, your stroke is not effective, and you have a higher score than you desire.

Now watch the professional. Yes, he or she is following a technique for swinging the club which matches what you have been told, but there is a difference. The professional is not obsessed with each detail. The professional is relaxed, placing the ball where it is desired by moving naturally, not constantly rattling off a series of mental steps needed to complete the perfect swing. You have been limited by your instructor making you obsessed with the details of what you do.

The Natural Way for Physical Activity

By this time, you are probably questioning my statement that the natural approach to the sport is the way to improve. After all, every game has certain hand positions to master, whether it is the way you grip your tennis racket or the way you throw a football. You naturally assume that only by concentrating on the details will you be skilled.

I want you to try an experiment right now. Get up. Yes, interrupt your reading for a minute and stand up. Then, when you are standing, walk around the room you are in, then sit down again.

No cheating, now. Walk around the room before going on with this book.

All finished? How did you keep your balance? Do you realize that you frequently were on one foot while the other was moving forward? Your toes, ankles, knees, and other joints all had to bend at critical times or you would have fallen on your face. You constantly had to make subtle shifts of your body so that you wouldn't have your weight in an awkward manner which could have made you topple to the floor. You had to spot the furniture and maneuver around it, again without shifting your weight in such a manner that you might fall.

The answer to how you could take that walk is simple. A professional walking coach taught you all you needed to know for this activity, right? You were taught how to be constantly aware of each slight movement of every joint in the body, right? You stood up, making certain your feet were on the floor. You pushed yourself both forward and upright, feeling every subtle change in your chest and head position in order to keep your balance. You knew that if you pushed too hard, your knees would lock and you would topple onto your face. If you kept your knees too loose and used too little force to stand erect, you would sit back down. But you thought about all these subtle nuances of balance, just as that highly paid professional walking coach taught you, and that's why you could walk around the room.

That isn't how it happened? You learned as a baby when there was no coach around? You practiced every day until standing and walking were automatic, then let your body take over? You concentrate now on whatever you are doing other than walking? Such a complex act, so extremely difficult, especially with the balance problem of being on only two legs (animals have four legs to help them remain steady), and you didn't think about it? In fact, had you thought about it, you would have been slower, awkward, perhaps fallen a few times? Is that an accurate description of your experience?

Congratulations. You are the most successful athlete around. You can stand and walk about, a feat requiring greater skill and learning than any sport you might deliberately try to master. And the key to your success is the way in which you used your subconscious mind.

The Skill of the Subconscious Athlete

Everything you routinely do with your body, you have programmed into your subconscious mind. This is the portion of the mind which can function automatically. When you first learn any skill, including walking, you must make conscious decisions about each step. Then, when it becomes second nature to you, you stop wasting your conscious awareness by always thinking about the action. You become more purposeful, accomplishing such actions as walking to the grocery store while consciously thinking of the items you are going to purchase.

Consider a sport such as football. You have to know how to throw the ball, catch the ball, and run evasively. Is that as complex as spotting your knife and fork, picking them up, using them to cut your meat to a bite-sized piece (remember that you have only your eyes and memory to determine which size is "bite-sized"), possibly transferring your fork to the other hand, setting down the knife, lifting the fork, knowing the distance to the center of your open mouth, putting the food inside, bringing your teeth to a level where the meat can be removed from the fork, replacing the fork on the table, chewing the food, sensing when it is swallowable, and then swallowing? More than a dozen skills have to be mastered in order to eat your food with a knife and fork. Approximately three true skills, not just bodily development and the learning of plays, have to be mastered to play football. Eating is far more difficult than mastering the athletic skill, but because we now have the techniques for eating placed in our subconscious mind, we do not see them as valuable abilities.

We routinely program our subconscious mind in a positive manner when we are learning new skills. We walk, talk, eat, drive a car, write a letter, and otherwise handle quite complex tasks easily and efficiently. We knew when we were younger that we wanted to be able to handle these chores, and so we learned them, placing the knowledge of these abilities into our subconscious. Now we can walk around the room, sit down to eat, or handle anything else without having to think about what we are doing.

Just as we can program the subconscious mind for positive actions, so we can also program it for negative thoughts. Remember at the start of this chapter when I told you all the reasons why various sports are difficult for you to learn? You probably agreed with what I was saying when you read it, didn't you? Yet as you read further, you realized that perhaps there was something wrong with those statements. Perhaps your attitudes were not based on the reality of becoming the best you can be in the sport of your choice.

Yet why have you felt such negative attitudes toward your learning abilities? Why have you let the television commercials, the hype of advertising, the promotions of equipment manufacturers so influence you? It is because they have programmed your subconscious mind for failure. You are saying, "I am going to run faster and longer than I did last week" when you take up jogging. But your subconscious mind is saying, "No way are you going to do that. You're a nobody who goes to school or has a job and jogs a few days a week. You can't be better than you are. You can't go further than you did last week. Only professional athletes improve, not you."

So what happens? You think positively when you start running. "I am going to do better than before. I am going to run faster and farther. I am not going to get winded so quickly." And off you go, knowing that your positive thinking will get you through.

Suddenly you spot the location where you normally become winded and tired. It is approaching faster and faster, but you are determined. "I can do it! I can do it!" you say to yourself. Then you hit the spot, the one your subconscious mind knows is the point where you must become exhausted, and you are drained. Your wind goes, you are tired, you try to push on, but it is no good. You are dragging yourself, panting hopelessly. "Maybe tomorrow," you tell yourself. "Maybe next week." And the subconscious laughingly says, "Maybe never, you fool!"

Why Aren't Professional Athletes Affected by the Subconscious?

Professional athletes have as many problems with their subconscious minds as anybody else. They program themselves for success, and they program themselves for failure, never recognizing the latter.

Perhaps the most obvious use of subconscious programming for defeat can be seen in professional boxers. The more prestigious the fight, the greater the prefight publicity. This publicity usually is presented in one of two ways: positive hype or negative hype.

"The Fight of the Century Approach" might be the title of a positive hype campaign. Each athlete is touted as being the greatest of the moment. "Never before in history have two such skilled heavyweights come together to determine which man is the greater boxer" is one example of the writing which occurs. The height, weight, arm reach, win-loss record, and other factors pertaining to each man are compared. The skills of past opponents, the ability to handle different fighting styles, and numerous other details are rehashed, always with the same conclusion: The men are equal. The battle will be determined by the amount of training, the concentration of the athletes, and luck.

What happens when both boxers read all this publicity? They recognize that this is the greatest challenge they have ever faced. They train harder than they have trained in their lives. They do more roadwork. They work out with the finest sparring partners they can find. They study films of their opponent's previous fights. And when they walk into the ring, each man is supremely confident of victory.

Such fights often go fifteen rounds and may be decided by points rather than by a serious knockout. A man may get knocked down, but he does not lose his confidence. He knows that he made an error in tactics, remembers the films of previous fights by his opponent, remembers the counter to the blow, and realizes he can now win. After all, his opponent, having scored a knockdown, will use that same method of fighting to try and score a knockout. But now the boxer is expecting that tactic, which gives him an edge. The knockdown was a good action. It brought the boxer to his senses and won't happen again. In other words, the subconscious, fueled by the press, is programmed only for victory.

"The Bum and the Champion Approach" is the opposite of the "Fight of the Century" campaign. Now the boxer is touted as "the greatest," and the other boxer is considered a joke. Perhaps the challenger's win-loss record is not very good. Perhaps the differences in arm reach, weight, and other factors are considered significant. Perhaps the champion has achieved such mythological proportions in the minds of the press that he is considered unbeatable at the moment. Whatever the case, the fight is a joke, a foregone conclusion, the challenger unable to win or the champion unable to keep his crown because he is past his prime. One man is good; the other is not up to the challenge.

Each day that passes brings an endless barrage of publicity which is favorable toward one fighter and unfavorable toward the other. The result can be a disaster because of the effect on the subconscious.

Most commonly, the "bum" in our scenario is convinced he is not as good. He is slightly tired in the morning during roadwork and thinks that he is a little more winded than usual after going five miles. Instead of recognizing that the ease of roadwork always varies from day to day, a natural fluctuation for all athletes, he decides that the slight loss of wind indicates he really is past his prime.

Then, during boxing, the sparring partner breaks through his defenses a couple of times. Again there is the subconscious fear—this time that if a sparring partner can hurt him, what will the champion do?

The challenger goes out to eat, his body lean and hard, so someone jokes that if he eats too many vegetables, he'll get flabby before the fight. "You don't want any more of a gut on you than you've got now" is the joke, a ridiculous idea for a man in such perfect physical shape. But again the challenger's subconscious is being primed, this time with negative message units saying, "You've let yourself get fat. Maybe you can't take punches in the stomach any more. How can you fight if you're flabby?"

Finally, the fight begins. The champion has been following his publicity and knows he will win easily. The challenger is already defeated by his fears. He will get winded. He can't handle too many stomach punches. He isn't the man he used to be. And on and on and on as the fight progresses. Then, when he loses, the press congratulates itself because it predicted the scenario everyone knew would happen.

In a similar scenario, the challenger, programmed to lose, gets in a lucky punch, sending the champion to the canvas. In that instant, the champion may get mad, decide to stop "toying" with the "jerk" who is challenging him, and proceed to tear him apart. At the same time, the challenger may recognize that it was a lucky punch, he has enraged the champion, and he will be lucky if he can simply ward off most of the blows before his inevitable defeat.

In some fights, quite the reverse happens. The lucky punch instantly reprograms the subconscious minds of both fighters. The champion realizes that he is not invulnerable. The press may have been wrong. He has a real fight on his hands, and he is not certain that he has trained hard enough to triumph. He becomes more cautious, less aggressive, and more vulnerable to attack. The challenger also has a change of attitude. If he, the "certain loser," can knock down the champion, maybe the champion isn't all that great. Maybe the press was wrong. He becomes the aggressor, more confident, suddenly aware that he can win this fight and determined to do so. Now the champion is programmed for failure, and the former "bum" is the skilled predator. And the press will enjoy writing about "The Upset of the Century."

What does all this mean to you? Your subconscious mind has been programmed for failure through no fault of your own. You have read how hard the sport(s) of your choice might be to master. You have reinforced that programming by playing with players better than yourself, thus assuring your defeat and frustration, or with players worse than yourself, telling yourself that "nobody" can play the game very well. You have not put the skills of the professionals and the time they devote to training in the proper context, as described earlier. And thus your subconscious mind is constantly destroying your determination to win and your belief in your ability to improve, and eliminating the chance for you to be the best which you are truly capable of being.

Fortunately, you need not remain a victim of your subconscious. The subconscious mind easily can be reprogrammed for success. In fact, among the thousands of patients I have treated over the years, a surprising number have been the professional athletes you have seen as sports idols. They have been suffering from negative programming of their subconscious minds. They have physical skills, great abilities, yet they "know" they will fail under certain conditions. (A younger opponent who is faster or an older opponent who has more experience. A clay court or grass court for tennis. Playing in the opponent's town instead of on home turf or playing at home when only "away" games can be won. And so the list grows.) They want me to help them reprogram their subconscious mind so they can do their best, winning or losing for reasons other than mental programming.

What I do for them is something I can do for you as well. You can learn to become the best player of which you are capable, utilizing the secret of the professionals. This change will occur gradually over time, but it will advance you beyond the level of your greatest expectations.

The Mind vs. the Body

There is one point that is important to stress. You cannot think your way to success if you do not first learn the game.

I am reminded of Professor Harold Hill in the play *The Music Man*. He was a con artist with no musical training. He sold the instruments necessary to equip a boys' band. Then he taught them to play by the "think method." The boys had only to think their way through a song, and somehow the music would come out sounding exactly as it should. Naturally, the music was terrible, the think method doing nothing but proving the gullibility of the boys and their parents.

In order for you to have my program work for you, you first must learn the basics of the sport you want to master. This means learning both the rules and strategies, but also practicing when you have the opportunity. I can show you how to reprogram your subconscious for success on the tennis court, for example, but you will not be successful unless you learn the correct method to hold the racket, complete a serve, and move along the baseline to be in a position to return the ball. I can teach you how to play golf with the confidence of a professional and growing skills constantly reducing your handicap. But first you must learn to hold the club and play some practice rounds.

Fortunately, this should not be a problem for you. Chances are excellent that you already have learned the sport(s) you want to master. You probably have taken some basic lessons, read a book or two, and/ or been taught the basics by a friend who plays. Yet your efforts have been frustrated by the fact that you are not very good and have not been able to improve. Since this is likely to be the case, you will be able to see almost immediate results from your reprogramming.

If by chance you are reading this book before taking up a new sport, you can program your mind for success even as you start your training. You will be able to accept the fact that you will not be perfect at the start. You will not become frustrated by the sometimes slow learning process while you train your body to handle the demands of the activity. And you will constantly move forward, advancing at a rate that is faster than you thought possible and, most likely, faster than the rate of those with the same training level as you.

The Role of Self-Hypnosis

The technique you will learn in the next chapter is that of self-hypnosis. This is the natural way to program your subconscious. It is not magic, nor will you be out of control while working with it. As you will learn, it is simply a method for focusing your mind and bypassing the negatives of conscious awareness. It is a technique anyone can use and one which is utilized in one form or another by almost all top athletes. They may call it "psyching themselves up" or some other term, but they are merely focusing on the problem at hand, then reprogramming their minds for success.

You have already been using self-hypnosis in a negative way without realizing it. How often have you read about an outstanding athlete in the sport you want to play better, only to say, "I'll never be like him (or her). I'll never be that good. I'll only be a bad player." Then you might add the reinforcement of thinking about the last bowling game, when you had almost all gutter balls, or about a golf score of 346, or about a tennis game where you had trouble getting the ball over the net while serving, only to lose every return, or about any other problem. You have been carefully programming your subconscious mind for failure, never realizing that fact.

Once you understand the basics of self-hypnosis outlined in the next chapter, you will find that succeeding chapters reveal how to use this new knowledge in a wide variety of sports. If the one you want to play better is not mentioned, you still will be able to adapt the concepts to your special needs. This is an approach which works with literally every sport, and this has been proven time and time again, both by me and by other therapists using this technique. You are going to have to adjust to being a winner in the future, an adjustment I suspect you will delight in making.

Now turn the page and begin learning the technique which will help you improve your skills beyond what you once thought was possible. Together we are going to help you triumph over all the negatives which have dominated your attempts to enjoy the sports you have so long admired.

The secret
of the pros

3

As you have seen, the programming of the subconscious mind is the greatest key to victory or the surest method of defeat for the athlete, whether beginner, advanced, or professional. All professional athletes attempt to manipulate their subconscious minds by getting "psyched up" for the game. Their methods vary, some being better than others. The most successful athletes—and many of them have come through my offices—work to reprogram their subconscious minds through the technique of self-hypnosis. It is this technique, this "secret" of the pros, that you will learn in this chapter. It will take a little time for practice, but once you have mastered it you can call upon it in seconds. Even more important, subsequent chapters will show you how to utilize it in any sport in which you want to participate.

Self-hypnosis is actually one of the most natural of mental states. The ability to use self-hypnosis is probably as old as civilization. Early humans would have utilized it much as we do today, though it was never called by this term until recent times. It is simply a means of focusing your mind toward a specific end without being distracted by the cares around you. At the same time, you are able to function perfectly normally, in full control of whatever is happening.

To give you an idea how self-hypnosis affects your conscious and unconscious mind, think about a time when you were in school and were concerned about a problem. It might have been a problem with a friend, a concern about a low grade you had to show your parents, or almost anything else. You left school, thinking intensely about the problem as you walked across the schoolyard. The schoolyard was filled with friends and acquaintances, but your thoughts were so concentrated that you never saw them. You simply walked toward home, aware only of the problem.

As you walked, you passed some students playing basketball. They were running around, and you moved so that you would not be hit. Baseball was also being played, and you moved across the field, dodging players, the ball, the runners, and others, never taking your mind from the concern you had.

You walked down the street, crossing safely when the traffic slowed properly, waiting when it didn't. Someone pulled out of a parking space without looking where he was going, and you managed to dodge the car without really being aware of it. You were totally preoccupied with your concern, yet you managed to avoid perhaps a dozen or more potentially dangerous situations. Your conscious mind was focused on the problem of greatest concern, and your subconscious mind handled the details of getting you home safely.

Or suppose you are on the job and you have been given an important assignment to complete the next day. You know that if you complete it effectively, you will be given a promotion or at least be more assured of your position within the company. If you make a mistake, you might as well forget advancing for a long time.

You get in a car and start to drive, thinking only of the assignment. You are not consciously paying attention to the traffic conditions, the freeway rush-hour congestion, your particular exit, or anything else. You are thinking only of your problem at work. Despite this, you speed up and apply your brakes at appropriate moments, you hit no one and alter your speed when someone is endangering you,and you make your exit, arriving home without incident.

There are numerous other incidents which occur every day in all of our lives in which we use this form of intense concentration, perhaps only for a few minutes at a time. We focus on the problem at hand, letting our conscious minds handle the concern and our subconscious minds automatically deal with everything else. We have tapped the same mental conditions you will use with self-hypnosis.

To show you the equivalent of this phenomenon in sports, think about a successful football quarterback. The quarterback's conscious mind has several concerns. First, he knows the person to whom he is to throw the ball. The receiver was designated in the play plan, and that is the quarterback's first concern. If the receiver is effectively blocked, he has an idea where other team members will be. Then, when he spots the first person who is open and whom he can reach with the ball, he fires a pass. If there is no one clear, he will take the ball and run to the goal. All of these decisions are conscious ones.

What is happening subconsciously? The quarterback is constantly aware of both teams and their manipulations around him. He may choose to run backwards to avoid tackles who have not been blocked, he may recognize he is about to be tackled and throw short to move the ball, he may see the players around whom he must run to make the goal if he can not pass the ball. There are dozens of decisions, endless body movements, and numerous changes in plan taking place in a matter of seconds as that quarterback prepares to throw the ball. Yet all of these are handled by the properly programmed subconscious mind.

What would happen if the subconscious was programmed for defeat, as can be a problem? The quarterback would know only one fact—the entire opposing team was out to tackle, crush, maim, and mutilate him. The natural reaction would not be to calmly analyze the field, pass the ball, or run toward the goal post. The natural reaction with the wrong subconscious program would be to run in the opposite direction as fast as possible to keep those eleven big bruisers from crushing him.

The following technique may seem a little involved when you first try it. However, it is a way of learning self-hypnosis which will be extremely effective for you in the future. You will not only be able to teach your subconscious mind to handle the technical side of sport, you will also be able to program yourself for improvement and success. You will find yourself constantly getting better, a success beyond your greatest expectations. You will be able to deliberately place yourself in a state of self-hypnosis each time you are preparing for a hard practice session or competition. In addition to the practical benefits of mastering this natural function of the human mind, you will also find it extremely relaxing. Just remember that you will need to practice the skill regularly, perhaps for a few minutes each day, so that it will become second nature to you.

The Relaxation Phase

Place yourself in a semicomfortable position. This may mean sitting upright on a comfortable chair or propped up on pillows in bed. You should select an approach which is not likely to put you to sleep. You will be extremely relaxed and can drift off to sleep easily. There is nothing wrong with doing this, but you will need to stay awake during the self-hypnotic induction if you are to learn this skill.

You want to remain aware, to be able to formulate suggestions. A completely comfortable position, such as lying flat on the bed, will most likely cause you to go to sleep. If you must stay on the bed, keep your head propped at least twelve inches above the level of your feet.

Whatever your position, take off your shoes so that you have air circulating around your feet. This will make you more sensitive, since there will be no constricting of a part of your body.

Now make yourself sensitive to your body. Move your body until you do not feel restricted by your clothing or any other physical discomforts. Think of yourself as floating free, unhampered in any way.

Once you are comfortable, think of your hands. This is the area where the greatest change in skin resistance takes place. Just by concentrating on your hands, you will feel some physiological changes taking place.

To demonstrate this to yourself as you are sitting comfortably, start at your hands. Attempt to feel some tingling sensation or numbness, almost as if whatever is inside of the skin is expanding and trying to get out of it. Now take your hand and place it back on your chair, continuing to be aware of this sensation or feeling. Does your hand feel cold or numb? Is it feeling overly relaxed? Is it heavy? Is it relaxed? Pick one word which best describes what you are feeling, and try to correlate the feeling with the word. Concentrate on your hand for approximately three to five minutes. When you sense the feeling growing stronger, say the word to yourself. For example, you might say, "I am feeling a cold, tingling sensation. . . . A tingling, cold sensation."

Now take the words *cold* and *tingling*, and try to decide which one you are feeling the most. Whichever word you select will become your physical key word. Of course, this can be any word which relates to your feeling. I am using *cold* and *tingling* for my example.

Once you have established your physical key, gently lay your hands across the top of your legs. Each time you think of that physical key word, you will think of that sensation.

Concentrate on the rest of your body, moving your attention to your arms, your shoulders, your thighs, and so forth, on to the bottoms of your feet. Each time you think of a new location, mention the key word and try to recall the same feeling that you had in your hands. In our example, you might think "cold" when concentrating on your ankles and the other parts of your body.

Once the physical key word sensation is achieved and controlled, the law of association becomes extremely strong. This means that when you say the word, you also sense the feeling which led you to select it originally. This fact will help you with the rest of the self-hypnosis conditioning process, which involves your emotional and intellectual keys.

As the physiological change takes place (you think the word "cold" while concentrating on a part of your body and you sense coldness there, for example) and your mind associates it with your physi cal key word, the psychological effect will begin to take place. The fact that you are controlling one aspect of your physical body allows your emotions to run free and leads to your second or emotional key.

Once you feel the first physiological change take place, you will say to yourself, "The tingling sensation causes relaxation to move into my toes, into my heels, into my ankles, and into the calves of my legs. I become aware of my legs pushing down and this tingling sensation moving back up into my thighs and my hips. I am aware of the contact between my hand and my thighs, and this tingling sensation will soon move upward into my arms. As I become aware of my stomach muscles relaxing, I become aware of this tingling sensation moving upward and I become aware of my breathing."

Since your breathing has a stronger effect on emotional change than any other function of your body, it should be used to establish and trigger your emotional key. Concentrate on your breathing until you feel it beginning to expand. Then try to become aware of your emotional feeling and attempt to tie in some positive word that can affect your emotional feelings at this moment. This will increase the strong effect of the law of association.

Keep in mind that you do not want to have any negative feelings or emotions. You should use only positive words, such as *happiness, success, confidence, peacefulness*, or whatever other word gives you a sensation of elation or well-being. Each time you say the word, pause and try to become aware of any emotion you can feel. For example, if the word is *happy*, you will tie in this word with the physical sensation of the expansion of your breathing and the drawing of new oxygen into the blood. Should this be the word you select, then *happy* will become your emotional key.

Finally, you will need the intellectual key. This is the third and most important of the key words for self-hypnosis. However, this word will be the same for everyone. You will either use "deep hypnotic sleep" or just "deep sleep."

Sleep is a basic human need. It is a condition to which we have been responding from the day we were born. We yield to this condition each night, allowing our minds to become inhibited and go almost blank for a few moments before drifting into the normal escape mechanism called sleep.

Your subconscious mind can only relate to a condition of habit. Thus each time you place yourself in this position to sleep, your subconscious mind assumes that you are going to sleep and your conscious mind is allowed to go into unconsciousness, drifting into a normal sleep.

During this period, your body is allowed to rest. More important, through dreams your mind is allowed to vent all the thoughts, traumas, ideas, and events which no longer have any value to you. Sleep then becomes an extremely strong intellectual conditioning. You cannot deny the fact that you can, will, and must sleep. Your intellectual suggestibility, which requires logic and reason, must respond to the suggestion of "deep sleep."

You will utilize this condition in self-hypnosis. However, you will alter a few of the factors which would normally put you to sleep in order to remain open to suggestion.

First, change the position of your body so that it is different from the position you would normally assume for sleep. This is why I suggested avoiding the bed or, if you must be in bed, keeping your head elevated at least twelve inches above your legs so that its level is different from that you would use for sleep.

Second, you will say either "deep hypnotic sleep" or just "deep sleep," since the word "deep" is not one normally used when at rest. This will help further distinguish between the two states.

In the beginning, the techniques described may place you only in a very light state of hypnosis. With repetition the suggestions will become more natural, the state of hypnosis will deepen, and you will feel a very strong response to the three key words.

Any stimulus played over and over in the mind soon becomes a habit or trigger mechanism. Experiments have been conducted on the creation of automatic trigger mechanisms to see how frequently a suggestion must be repeated and practiced before it is a part of the subconscious. We have discovered that with twenty-one repetitions under hypnosis, any condition placed properly in the mind becomes a trigger mechanism with ever growing strength.

During your early practice sessions, you may find yourself experiencing the preliminary aspects of sleep. You may start to sense the rapid eye movement of the dream state or even have your eyes start to roll up under the eyelids. You should encourage this condition by letting your eyes roll up, at the same time repeating the words "deep hypnotic sleep." This will develop the natural law of asssociation between the rolling of the eyes and the words "deep hypnotic sleep."

There are many myths about hypnosis. One of these is that you are giving up all control and conscious awareness when you are hypnotized, by yourself or others. The truth is quite different, though. Thus, you may be surprised to find that you have full conscious awareness when you have entered this hypnotic state. Do not be concerned. A person in a natural state of self-hypnosis always retains full conscious awareness. This is your clue to the fact that you are in the hypnotic state rather than the normal sleep state.

On television and in novels, someone who is hypnotized seems to drop into a deep, black whirlpool or perhaps to experience some dramatic sounds. Bells may ring, lightning flashes, and the world seems to change somehow. Yet none of this occurs in reality. It is a natural condition over which you have full control, and does not result in such sound and fury.

While in self-hypnosis, you will hear everything around you. You will have full conscious awareness, though you will feel a little as you do when awake and daydreaming. You will be relaxed and may feel slightly detached from those all around. Your mind may wander, and you may feel a numbness or tingling in your fingers or toes.

You may also forget the subject on which you wanted to concentrate. This is no problem. In such a relaxed state, it is natural for your mind to wander. The important step is for you to learn the self-hypnosis technique and to practice until the condition becomes automatic.

Self-Hypnosis Conditioning: Summary

Assuming that your key words are *tingling, happy* and *deep hypnotic sleep,* you will place yourself in a semicomfortable position. Your hands will be resting on your thighs. As you concentrate on your hands, you will feel a tingling sensation in them. The tingling sensation will move down your body and into your legs.

Once it reaches your feet, you will then reverse the action, suggesting that you will feel this tingling sensation move into your toes, your heels, your ankles, the calves of your legs, moving upward to the area where there is contact between your hands and your legs, and then upward through your midsection.

As this relaxation begins to move upward into your stomach muscles and solar plexus, you become aware that it continues up through your arms. At this point you will concentrate upward to your breathing and place all your attention on your breathing. As this happens, say your emotional key word silently to yourself. In our example, the word is *happy,* and it will begin to represent the condition of your emotional state.

Continue to be aware of your breathing as the relaxation continues to move through your shoulders, up your back, into your neck muscles, through your scalp, and across your forehead. As it begins to move down through your facial muscles and jaw muscles, you become aware that your eyes have a tendency to roll upward under the lids.

As you recognize this upward movement of the eyes, plant the words *deep hypnotic sleep* over and over in your mind. This will strengthen the natural law of association.

The Awakening Procedure

Before going any further, it is important to become aware of the awakening procedure. This involves a series of steps you will use to bring yourself out of the hypnotic state. It is a very important part of any hypnotic suggestion.

The awakening procedure is meant to create a condition in which you are brought fully out of the hypnotic state. Without this procedure, you will remain for a period of time in a highly suggestible state. You will be suggestible not only to your own thoughts but to the stimuli all around. This means that if many negative ideas are presented, you might let these have great power over your actions. Since you are learning self-hypnosis in order to have more positive personal growth in your athletic endeavors, you want to be certain to avoid any chance at increasing negative ideas.

The awakening procedure involves creating a condition which your mind will associate with awakening. The best procedure is to count from zero to five ("0, 1, 2, 3, 4, 5") and say the words "wide awake." After you have placed yourself in a hypnotic state a few times, then brought yourself out of it, you will begin to recognize the feelings associated with each state. This will probably not occur at first as you are learning, but be assured that both stages are occurring.

When entering the state of hypnosis, some people have what they report as a twinge of current passing over their foreheads. Others say that they have a sense of numbness or a sense of calm. Whatever you experience, and it may be quite different from these states, there will be a definite reaction which you can sense.

There is also a change upon awakening. This may be a slight trembling or a renewed alertness. Again, each person is likely to be somewhat different, but everyone feels something specific. These feelings are important because you will always be aware of when you are in or out of self-hypnosis.

While you are learning self-hypnosis to help your athletic abilities, you will want to practice daily. This practice should be deliberate and separate from your workouts and practice time. You may want to use the practice to prepare yourself for a game or other competition, giving yourself whatever suggestions are appropriate for the particular sport, but it should be attempted each day regardless of the purpose. Ideally, this will also mean spending at least fifteen minutes each day in the self-hypnotic condition.

There is a chance that you will be disturbed during your practice. Ideally, you will learn self-hypnosis while alone at home or in some other quiet location. But even under the best of circumstances, the telephone might ring, there may be a knock at the door, or, if you are outside, someone may pass. The moment you are disturbed, be certain to count yourself out ("0, 1, 2, 3, 4, 5, wide awake"). Just because your eyes are open, you are walking around, and you are aware of all that is going on does not mean that you are out of the hypnotic state. You are actually continuing to be open to both positive and negative suggestions from your own thoughts and the statements of those around you. This is especially bad when you consider the fact that there are more negative suggestions on the news, in newspapers, and in everyday life than positive suggestions, thus giving you the risk of experiencing anxiety and mild depression.

If you notice these symptoms and remember that you had not taken yourself out of hypnosis, you can easily correct this problem. Go through the procedure for entering self-hypnosis, then count yourself out, being certain to end with the words *wide awake*.

The degree of hypersuggestibility you can develop will vary with the individual. Some men and women report that they are quite skilled in self-hypnosis after a day and are able to apply it easily to their sports activities almost immediately. Others take a week, and still others take months to truly be able to work quickly on entering. However, right from the start everyone is able to begin changing his or her subconscious. Complete mastery, which may take many weeks for some, is *not* a factor in your ability to improve your athletic ability. Once you are able to enter the self-hypnotic state, and you will do that the first time you try the approach outlined, you will begin improving your bowling average, golf score, tennis game, baseball skills, etc. You will be able to correct any problems which might exist and make your current workout sessions and competition better than you ever thought possible for your current skill level.

A Self-Hypnosis Induction

Now that you understand how to induce self-hypnosis, this section will show you how you will talk yourself through the hypnotic state. In the next chapter, you will begin learning how to apply the hypnosis so that you can radically improve your athletic ability, no matter what your current level of proficiency.

Start by placing yourself in a semicomfortable position as described. Have your shoes off, and move about until you feel that you are unencumbered and free. Your hands should be resting on your thighs, your eyes closed, your mind drifting over your entire body.

Concentrate on your hands. Say your physical key word, and allow yourself to feel the change taking place. Now say:

"I begin to feel this sense of physical relaxation moving from my hands, into my thighs, going down through my knees, into the calves of my legs ... moving down into my ankles, to my feet, right up to my toes, relaxing my feet completely.

"Now I concentrate on this relaxation at the tip of my toes, moving down toward my heels, up to my ankles, through the calves of my legs, up to my knees. And I feel the sensation of relxation moving through my thighs, through my hips, all the way up to my waist, relaxing the entire lower half of my body now.

"I concentrate on my stomach muscles relaxing. I feel that I am letting go, allowing them to become very loose, very limp, just letting go. I concentrate on this relaxation moving up to my chest area, and I become aware of my breathing.

Now inhale, and say your second, emotional key word to yourself. Feel this emotional change taking place.

"I concentrate on this relaxation moving under my arms, going up in my back, encasing my entire back. I feel my back pressing down as I relax, and I allow this relaxation to move up, into my shoulders. My shoulders become very limp and loose, just like a rag doll, relaxing.

"I concentrate on this relaxation, moving from my shoulders, into my neck, relaxing all of my muscles, relaxing every fiber, every nerve and tissue in my neck, completely relaxing them now. I concentrate on this relaxation moving up into my head area, relaxing my entire head.

"First I relax all my facial muscles, my jaw muscles, I allow the slight separation of my lips, and I feel a slight dryness. The urge to swallow is taking place." (This is very normal with self-hypnosis.)

"I concentrate on this relaxation moving into my eye-lids,and my eyes have a tendency to roll up under my eyelids." At this point you say your intellectual key word to yourself.

"I concentrate on this relaxation moving into my scalp, my fore-head relaxing, allowing the blood to circulate very freely, very close to the skin now, with every breath I exhale.

"I go deeper into relaxation now. Deeper. Deeper. And with every breath I inhale, I welcome this relaxation. And as I exhale, I let go, going deeper and deeper into hypnosis, enjoying every moment now, enjoying every second as I go deeper and deeper.

"I begin to feel this inner peace, this inner calmness, and I like this feeling. And I'm going to allow this inner calmness to carry over into my daily life and become part of my life."

Now repeat your three key words to yourself and say, "Each time I say these words, I will sleep soundly and deeply. Each time I will go deeper than the time before."

Now imagine yourself standing at the top of a staircase, looking down twenty steps. "As I count from twenty down to zero, each number will represent a step taking me deeper into relaxation, deeper into self-hypnosis.

"Now I begin going down. Twenty, 19, 18, 17, 16, 15, 14, deeper and deeper now. Thirteen, 12, 11, 10, 9, 8, deeper and deeper now. Seven, 6, 5, 4, 3, 2, 1. Deeper asleep now. Deeper. Deeper.

"Now that I am learning to control this state of self-hypnosis, I begin to feel that I have a definite advantage over most people. I have access to my subconscious mind, the most powerful part of my mind. I can feel and be only the way I want to feel and be.

"And I can also now suggest to myself that I will accept only positive thoughts and ideas that are beneficial to me for my well-being and self-improvement. I have the ability to reject all negative thoughts, ideas, suggestions, or inferences from anyone, and I am developing more control over my mind and body.

"Each and every time I encounter a situation where, in the past, I became tense, nervous, upset, or fearful, I will find now that I am more relaxed, calmer, more confident, more sure of myself. I have the ability to handle situations so much better than ever before.

"Now in a few moments I am going to awaken myself. I am going to count from zero to five, and when I reach five I will open my eyes and I will awaken completely and totally. Physically I will be very relaxed, emotionally very calm, very peaceful, and very happy. Mentally, I will feel very sharp, very alert, thinking very clearly. And then I will place myself in the hypnotic state again, strengthening my conditioning, going into self-hypnosis.

"Zero, 1, 2, slowly and gently coming up now. Three, feeling more refreshed, more relaxed, feeling like I have had hours of restful sleep. Four, and *four* becomes a very alert number for me. I begin to feel my breathing changing, the movement in my eyes taking place. Almost awake now. Five. I'm wide awake. Wide awake now. Wide awake.

"Now that I'm in a semicomfortable position, my hands on my thighs, I concentrate on my physical key word, saying it to myself. I am feeling this physical sensation of relaxation moving from my hands, to my thighs, moving down into my knees, the calves of my legs, relaxing the calves of my legs completely.

"I am feeling the weight of my legs pressing down now. As this relaxation moves down into my ankles, into my feet, down into my heels, and then into my toes, my feet relax completely. I concentrate on this relaxation, reversing from my toes, moving through my heels, up through my ankles, moving through the calves of my legs, relaxing every muscle, every nerve, every fiber, every tissue in my leg, allowing the blood to circulate very freely. It is very close to the skin, unrestricted, as all of the muscles and nerves relax.

"This sensation of relaxation moves through my knees, in through my thighs, in through my hips, all the way up to my waist and mid-section. I concentrate on my stomach muscles relaxing. With every breath I exhale, I feel the muscles letting go, relaxing them very deeply.

"This concentration of relaxation now moves up into the chest muscles, and I become aware of my breathing. I become aware of every time I inhale and every time I exhale. I feel the movements of my body as I inhale and exhale.

"And as I inhale, I say my emotional key word to myself [say the word], implanting that word very deeply into my mind. And I allow the sensation of relaxation to move up into my shoulders, allowing them to feel very limp, loose, just like a rag doll.

"I feel the weight of my arms, and I become aware of how my arms are hinged to my shoulders. And then my shoulders relax. I allow my arms to relax, feeling the weight of my arms pressing down.

"I concentrate on this relaxation moving down from my shoulders, down into my back. I relax my entire back now, relaxing it completely. This relaxation moves into my neck, and I relax every fiber, every muscle, every nerve and tissue in my neck. Deeply relaxing my neck.

"I feel this relaxation moving up into my head, starting with my jaw and jaw muscles. I allow my jaw to relax completely until I feel a slight parting of my lips. A dryness takes place on my lips, and soon the urge to swallow will follow.

"And then I concentrate on all my facial muscles relaxing together now. This relaxation moves up to my eyes and my eyelids. As I begin to relax my eyelids, I begin to sense my eyes have a tendency to roll upward. And as this takes place, I say _____ [use your last key word] and I go deep, deep asleep.

"This relaxation works up into my forehead, and I allow this relaxation to move into my scalp, relaxing all my scalp muscles, allowing the blood to circulate and move freely, very close to the skin.

"I am relaxing my entire head now, and as the relaxation invades my entire body, from my toes all the way up to my head, and from my head all the way down to my toes, I feel like a peaceful, pleasant blanket of relaxation has passed over me. And with every breath I exhale, I continue to go deeper and deeper into hypnosis, deeper into relaxation. I begin to feel the positive sensation of relaxation of my entire being. I begin to welcome this relaxation with every breath I inhale. And as I exhale, I allow myself to go deeper and deeper, deeper and deeper.

"In a few moments, I am going to take myself deeper into this state. I begin to imagine myself standing at the top of a staircase, looking down. Each number represents another step, going deeper and deeper into hypnosis, deeper and deeper into relaxation. And when I reach zero, I will be deeper than ever before.

"Now I begin going down. Twenty, 19, 18, 17, 16, 15, 14, 13, 12, 11, 10, deeper and deeper now. Nine, 8, 7, 6, going down. Five, 4, 3, going all the way down. Two, 1, 0, and deeper asleep now. Deeper and deeper.

"Now I allow my mind to drift over my entire body, and I feel this relaxation becoming more prominent. I am enjoying every moment now, as I go deeper and deeper, knowing I am gaining more and more control over my mind and body. I have access to the most powerful part of my mind, my subconscious, so I can choose the way *I* want to feel, so I can become the way *I* want to become. I know that my mind is receptive to positive thoughts, ideas, and directions which give me a feeling of the way *I* want to become. I know that my mind is receptive to positive thoughts, ideas, and directions which give me a feeling of well-being. And each time I use my formula and desire to enter this state, I go in quickly, soundly, and deeply.

"Each time I will go deeper than the time before, knowing that this condition becomes stronger with each passing day.

"In a few moments, I am going to suggest to myself that I will accept only positive thoughts and ideas that are beneficial to me for my well-being, for my self-improvement. I will have the ability to reject all negative thoughts, ideas, or inferences from anyone. And each time I approach a situation where I became, in the past, nervous, tense, upset, or fearful, I will now find that I am more relaxed, calmer, more confident, and more sure of myself. And I begin to like myself more.

"And now as I become aware of this peacefulness and this calmness, I find I like this feeling. I like this feeling so much, I am going to hold on to this feeling. Nothing and no one will take this feeling from me, because it belongs to me. This control over my mind and body belongs to me.

"And now I am going to imagine I am watching a clock, watching the second hand ticking away. Starting at number twelve, as it ticks away, I begin to realize that every second of hypnosis will represent to me many minutes of peaceful rest and relaxation where my mind and body become rejuvenated, regenerated, knowing that there is harmony between mind, body, and personality now. And this harmony will carry over into my daily life. I will be able to express myself more easily and naturally, be able to say what I feel like saying and do what I feel like doing, using my awakening process, counting from zero to five. With each number, I will become more and more awake. Physically I will be relaxed. Emotionally I will feel calm, peaceful, and happy. Mentally I will feel very sharp and very alert, thinking very clearly.

"And now I begin to awaken myself. Zero, 1, 2, slowly and gently coming up. Three, feeling more relaxed as I awaken. Four, and *four* becomes a very alert number. I begin to feel my breathing changing; the movement of my eyes taking place. And now, 5. Wide awake. Wide awake. Wide, wide, wide awake."

The stress
of pleasure

4

You have learned some of the mental attitudes which affect your subconscious mind, but what you may not realize is that athletic competition can trigger many of the reactions experienced with unpleasant events. Before looking at individual sports where you will utilize the techniques learned in Chapter 3, let us explore what I call the stress of pleasure.

The Fight-or-Flight Syndrome

Our bodies were designed for survival. Our earliest ancestors were raised in a world quite different from our own. There were no cars or planes. In many parts of the world, the horse had not been domesticated so riding was impossible. Men and women moved on their feet, often walking through dense brush where large wild animals waited to pounce. Weapons either did not exist or were crude, such as heavy sticks broken from trees and large rocks picked up from the ground. Even worse, humans were frequently slower and weaker than the creatures who thought they might make an ideal supper.

Obviously, early humans did not completely perish in these encounters. Otherwise we would be just another species that had gone our evolutionary way. Instead we were provided with a great weapon—the fight-or-flight syndrome.

The biological activities which occur when the fight-or-flight syndrome takes place are not important. Adrenalin flows, and you suddenly find that you are better able to handle the crisis. Your mind is suddenly sharper, your body stronger, and your movements quicker than normal. You are ready to tackle the creature which has designated you as its next meal (*fight*) or to race in the opposite direction, climb a tree, or otherwise elude the animal (*flight*).

All these changes can be channeled effectively or ineffectively, depending upon your training and experience. A giant saber-toothed tiger might attack one man who flails helplessly at the animal, striking with fists and feet until the tiger's jaws crush the life from his body. The man is stronger and fights more fiercely than he ever has before, but it is not enough to help him defeat the more powerful animal.

Later, a second man is attacked by the same animal. This time the man is someone who has observed the way the saber-toothed tiger hunts and kills. He has studied the animal's movements and has seen where it is most vulnerable.

This second man is being stalked by the tiger, only now he gathers a long, pointed stick in his hands. His adrenalin is pumping through his body, but he concentrates on the task at hand. Suddenly the tiger leaps, and the man moves to the side, positioning the stick so that the tiger will land with his full weight on the point. The stick punctures the tiger's throat, seriously wounding it.

Then the man grabs a rock and jams the rock between the animal's jaws. His arms are powerful, and the crude weapon severely chokes the tiger. The man is able to flee, climbing a tree, watching as the mortally wounded animal dies in agony.

Why did one man live and the other die when the fight-or-flight response gave both of them the same chance? It was because the one man was prepared. He had studied the potential danger and readied himself to do battle. Each move was carefully made so that all the force of his body could be channeled into the attack. His mind was programmed for victory, his subconscious utilizing the fight-or-flight syndrome to help him triumph.

How does all this relate to your sports activity? The fight-or-flight syndrome occurs in athletics, just as it does in matters of life or death. When you are standing alone by a bowling lane, holding the ball for the throw, knowing that friends are watching, you have the same type of reaction. If you are on the tennis court, waiting for the serve return, on a football field with players running all around, or almost anywhere else, the fight-or-flight syndrome takes place. When you have programmed your subconscious for effective action, you stand a better chance of winning than when you are not prepared. This is why some players "clutch" in a tight situation and others are able to perform to the best of their ability.

The fight-or-flight syndrome affects different athletes in different ways. Some golfers experience it every time they tee off. They are concerned that the ball will not go far enough, that it will go in the wrong direction, or that they will miss entirely. Their subconscious mind is prepared for mistakes, humiliation, and failure. It is screaming their amateur or beginner status at them. It is reminding them of past failures and the potential laughter of those playing with them. Their adrenalin flows, their muscles tighten, their breathing may change, and they might even have momentarily blurred vision. And the result is a flubbed drive.

Other golfers have no trouble with their drive. They have learned the basics of the swing and which club to use, and are quite relaxed. The ball goes in the right direction, and the distance varies with their body strength, the wind, and other factors. Yet they never experience the fight-or-flight syndrome until . . . the dreaded putt.

It is on the green that this type of golfer suddenly experiences the same internal reactions as he or she would if a saber-toothed tiger were lurking about the water hazard. "I'll hit the ball too far." "I'll hit the ball too hard." "It will bounce out of the hole." "It will take me too many strokes." "I'll knock it sideways." And on and on and on. Yet the player who clutched while teeing off may be completely relaxed on the green, having practiced putting so much that the subconscious mind is saying, "Well, at least this is something you can do well. I'm just surprised you ever got the ball this far, you hacker."

This situation happens with professional golfers all the time. One player breezes through putts but sweats other aspects of the game.

Another player comes close to a hole in one with every drive, then regularly misses what, for other golfers, would be easy putts.

Sometimes the fight-or-flight syndrome occurs because of anxiety created in unusual ways. For example, a baseball player enjoys a Little League game, a high school season, a college game, or perhaps an office softball team. Week after week the games take place and the player is always relaxed, enjoying the friendship, the exercise, and the skills being developed. There is little stress and tension because the games are for fun.

Suddenly everything changes for one game. Perhaps it is the championship playoffs or a high school team is playing its archrival. An office team may have a grudge match against a different department. Whatever the cause, the players are constantly exposed to such ideas as "This is the game that *really* matters," "All the other games were practice sessions for this all-important rivalry," "You can throw away the season record books for this match because anything goes with such an important event."

You have undoubtedly heard such hype before all-star games, Bowl games, Superbowl games, and similar events, both amateur and professional. The reality is that the game is the same, it will be played identically to how it has been played in the past, and the difference in the teams means very little. Yet the subconscious statements are slowly building intense pressures. You come to believe that the game is different, that all your experiences mean nothing, and that you cannot possibly be fully prepared. Your anxiety creates the fight-or-flight syndrome, which has not existed until that moment.

No matter what the sport, you can see how you, at times, work against yourself by letting the fight-or-flight response get out of control. You become your own worst enemy with a programmed subconscious overwhelming whatever training and experience you have had.

Negative Self-Hypnosis

You learned in the previous chapter about how to create a change in your subconscious mind through the use of self-hypnosis. If you will think back to what you have read, you will realize that many of the problems discussed in this chapter, difficulties everyone experiences regardless of sport, are a form of self-hypnosis. You are focusing your mind on the negative, shutting out all other mental stimulation, concentrating almost exclusively on failure.

The result of this hypnotic effect is that you are likely to perfect your greatest fear. For example, suppose you are standing at a bowling alley lane, thinking of a gutter ball. You consciously do not want a gutter ball. You consciously want to roll that ball perfectly into the pocket. It is only your subconscious mind which keeps shrieking "Gutter ball! Gutter ball!" The problem is that your body is responding to that subconscious thought, and your hand is slowly changing its angle to reflect what your subconscious desires. You aim perfectly for the gutter, rolling your way to defeat just as you programmed yourself to do.

The same situation exists with every other sport. Whatever you are creating within the subconscious will be reflected in the action you take, no matter what you consciously desire. The anxiety becomes hypnotic, reinforcing the most powerful force available, your subconscious mind.

The Other Negative Consequences of Anxiety

Some athletes find that their anxiety affects them in ways which can be literally injurious to their activity. They may tense, causing avoidable injuries such as sprained or broken arms or legs. They stiffen when they should relax, damaging their bones. Or they make themselves sick.

"I used to love long-distance running in gym class," said Mary, an enthusiastic amateur runner. "Our teacher would just let us run the whole period. We could leave the school grounds and go running past the houses and through a nearby park. So long as we didn't stop, we could go anywhere we wanted. I used to keep pushing myself, trying to go farther, faster, in the time we had. I was always relaxed.

"Every couple of weeks we'd have these races against each other. All the girls in my class would have to run over a set course to see who was the fastest. I had run that distance many times, but I never adjusted to having to race against someone else. Just before we'd start to run, I used to have trouble breathing and get sick to my stomach. I was always fine when I ran alone, and I didn't think I took the competition very seriously, but I always got sick. I never could do my best, and a couple of times I must have looked really awful because the teacher told me to sit down instead of running. I knew it was just my anxiety, but that never stopped my being sick."

One other problem of being anxious about some aspect of your game is that you lose sight of your abilities. You can become so focused on what you have yet to master that you forget where you have your skills.

For example, many tennis players worry that they do not have a strong serve. It goes over the net in bounds but is always returned by their opponents, even though they are not always able to return their opponents' stronger serves. The serve then becomes the focal point of their anxiety, and they stop making use of their strong points.

"I had great instruction when I was learning tennis," said Lynne. "I was taught how to race back and position myself for the return of a ball after I hit it. I was shown how to place it where my opponent would have the most difficult time returning it. I learned how to throw my opponent off balance with my return, but I never was very good with my serve.

"At first I could hold my own. I never won a serve, but when the balls were returned I could often run my opponents ragged chasing the balls all over the court, yet knowing where I should be to return them with control. I've played against some great players who beat me 6–0 when they controlled the serve. But when I served and was able to make returns, they would fight to beat me even though they were better overall.

"Then I got to worrying about my serve. It wasn't getting any better, and I was still having trouble mastering the hard, fast serves coming at me. I began spending all my time worrying about my serve, and pretty soon there were times I couldn't even get it over the net. I was better when I was just lobbing the ball, and I became so worried I forgot to concentrate on my returns, which I used to do well. Pretty soon I was losing heavily no matter who was serving. I had worried about one part of my game so much that the rest of the game suffered."

Lynne's experience is not unique. I have known bowlers who were so concerned with their approach that they stopped concentrating on the power and control which gave them an edge when they released the ball. I have seen basketball players so spooked by a bad lay-up shot that their skill in moving down the court and eluding their opponents began to slack off. Your anxiety can create the hypnotic effect which results in your focusing on one negative experience and forgetting the positive abilities which can make you a formidable player overall.

You may be wondering by now why I call this chapter "The Stress of Pleasure." This is because all the amateur and professional athletes with whom I have worked to improve their skills truly love their activities. They are having problems they want to master because athletic pursuits are fun.

The difficulty comes when we are in competition. Some people are able to see competition as completely enjoyable. They do not care whether they win or lose. If they are better than their opponents, they still try to use all their skills as a way of maintaining their abilities. If their opponents are better, they like to separate their emotions from the competition so they can observe how they are defeated, learning new techniques which will help their play. They do not feel that they must win or that they are worth less as individuals if they come out second best. They simply delight in playing, regardless of the circumstances.

Other people have all the enjoyment of sports except when they are in competition. They often have been raised with the misguided notion that their value as persons depends upon whether they win or lose on the athletic field. The idea of competition brings to mind parental lectures on the need to be Number One. They might remember some gym teacher who scorned anyone who wasn't a champion. Sometimes these influences were those of a seriously misguided adult who was never happy with his or her own life. At other times the adult chose the wrong words to try and influence a sensitive child, building fear instead of positive motivation and the acceptance of human differences. Whatever the case, the anxiety now dominates in competition.

Whether your stress of pleasure is positive, a simple adrenalin flow that helps you do your best even if your best means you will be in last place, or whether it is negative, you can learn to control it. You are capable of taking charge of your subconscious mind so that you can relax and improve.

Fortunately, you are not in the position of some athletes who find that the anxiety becomes so great that they simply give up a sport they might otherwise come to love. In such cases the endless frustrations, the constant reinforcement of failure, and all the other problems can make both amateurs and professionals abandon sports.

Should you be worried, this is not a problem for you. The fact that you are reading this book means that you have a positive mental attitude toward the sport(s) you are trying to master. Yet I suspect that no matter what sport you enjoy, you probably recognized some of your problems in this chapter. You can see that it is your subconscious mind which is making the difference between your present skills and the potentially unlimited skills you can achieve with a combination of practice and the reprogramming of your subconscious. Thus, let us look at a variety of sports, the difficulties which occur as you attempt to master them, and the ways you can use your new knowledge of self-hypnosis to speed this process.

Tennis

5

Sometimes it seems that tennis isn't a game, it is a reflection of life. The professional players fall into a number of different categories. First come the spoiled brats, the little boys and girls who have discovered that temper tantrums will usually get them anything they want. They curse the baseline judges, they shout obscenities at the crowd, they slam their rackets, and they challenge each call as though their entire future is dependent upon whether the ball is in or out.

Then there are the sophisticates. They wear tennis clothes the way some people wear evening gowns. They appear to be playing with a sterling silver racket in one hand, a martini in the other, and a designer original sweatband on their brow. Each move is perfected grace and, despite the band, not a drop of moisture is allowed on their foreheads.

There are also the hard-working professionals, the ones who see making a million dollars a year on the courts as a serious job. They come to work in a beat-up old Porsche, carrying several disreputable rackets. They arrive early to practice, step on the court precisely on time, and play almost machinelike, as though they have been programmed for serving, returning the balls, running, and winning. These are the people who usually marry, have families, and look upon being a tennis great the same way that someone else might view working on an assembly line.

The tennis zealots are the ones who see tennis as a religious experience and view their essential goodness as being determined by whether they win or lose. If they are able to run to the net and slam a tennis ball down the throat of their opponent, obviously God is on their side. They may become mystical, discussing the yin and yang of the racket, repeating a mantra between serves, and speaking unto the fans while sitting in a lotus position. Or they may become almost violent, their eyes glazed in the sunlight, slamming the ball back across the net as though it was sin incarnate and they were Christ, battling the money-changers in the temple.

For those of us who enjoy tennis as amateurs, be we beginners or advanced, our behavior is not so eccentric as that of the professionals, but it often reflects our emotions. Have you ever heard someone who was having a hard time in school or business talk about going over to the courts to slam a few tennis balls around? The court becomes an arena for coping with extreme anger and frustration.

Then there is the player who is forever apologetic. This is the individual who has a limited sense of self-worth and is constantly reinforcing failure. "I always hit the ball into the net. I'm such a dumb player, I don't know why you want to play with me." "Sorry I missed that shot. I never can get back to the baseline in time." "Sorry about that serve. I always get frustrated when it's my turn and hit the ball over the fence." "I'm dumb . . ." "I blew it . . ." "I'm sorry . . ." "I don't know . . ." "I can't . . ." Negative. Negative. Negative.

Magic players are also common. "I could win if I had the same racket (name your favorite pro) used when he/she beat _____ at Wimbledon [or Forest Hills or wherever]." "I never win when I wear this blouse. It's my loser blouse, but the good-luck blouse I've got needs washing, and I haven't had time." "It's the balls. You know I never can win with this brand. But the store was out of the good ones, and I had to settle for these." "What I really need is a different brand of tennis shoes. I can never seem to move right when I wear these, but they were all I could afford, and they do have the name of _____ [name a star player] written on the side, so I thought I'd take a chance. But they just aren't like the ones with _____ [name a different star] name on them.

I could really play well with those." On and on. Tennis can be won through magic but not through skilled play.

Then there are the indecisive players. "I've got to go for his/her backhand. That's his/her weak point. I'll play to the backhand and win. . . . Unless maybe I should try rushing the net. I've never rushed the net before so that will confuse my opponent. That's what I'll do. Never mind the backhand, I'll rush the net. . . . Unless maybe I should be placing my shots differently. Maybe get them real close to the base-line opposite where my opponent is going. Run that sucker ragged. That's the best strategy. . . . Unless. . . . My opponent's point? How could it be my opponent's point? That gives my opponent the game. How could that happen? I had my strategy so well planned. I was going for the backhand or the net or the placement or . . . I had strategy. Honest."

There are other types, of course, but I think you get the idea. If you have not seen yourself in all of this, you have probably recognized someone with whom you have played. In every case, the individual has created all the manner of subconscious programming guaranteed to cause failure, poor playing, and frustration.

What Is Tennis, Really?

Tennis, like all sports, is a game. It is a method for having fun, getting exercise, and relaxing with someone else. Unless you are a professional, winning or losing does not matter, though all of us enjoy triumphing over an opponent in such a game.

Tennis is also a sport which you can enjoy at any age. There are people in their seventies and eighties who enjoy the game, as well as preteens who spend their spare time on the tennis courts. There are indoor tennis courts in communities which have snow in winter and year-round courts outdoors in the sunbelt. Expenses are generally limited to the price of a racket and balls, since many courts are open to the public at no charge.

Tennis is not something magical. It is not a method for acting out your aggressions. And your skill is not a sign of your self-worth.

Tennis is fun, and mastering it through self-hypnosis is actually a matter of redirecting your subconscious so you have a more positive, realistic view of the game. Each time you have been focusing on the winning, on your anger, on the negatives of where you are weak in your play, you have been needlessly working against yourself.

Relaxation, the First Step to Winning

Relaxation is essential for every sport, but with tennis the chance of being injured is actually greater than with many other activities. If you are tense when you swing your racket, you may injure your arm or elbow. If you move about the court while under stress, you are likely to be stiff, hurting your knees, turning your ankles, or otherwise sustaining short- or long-term discomfort.

Relaxation is also critical for control of the ball. A serve must be relaxed in order to have maximum power and speed. The looping action of the serve needs to be smooth in order to insure that the ball goes where you want it, as fast as you can place it over the net. The same is true with your return. A tense player runs jerkily to where the ball is coming, does not have time to get into a good position, then swings with the elbow bent improperly. There is neither power nor control of the ball which, though it may go back over the net, usually is in just the position your more relaxed opponent desires for a devastating return.

Even your ability to sustain play is determined by your relaxation. Tension causes difficulty in breathing, less oxygen getting to your brain, and fatigue setting in much earlier than it should. No one can play his or her best when tired, so the ability to relax is a key factor for maintaining your stamina and maximum alertness.

How to Relax

There are several ways to relax, the most effective being the one you learned in Chapter 3 in conjunction with the information about self-hypnosis. This is a variation of what is known as fractional relaxation. You are concentrating on each portion of your body until you have relaxed your entire body. It is a way to relax you can do at home, in the locker room, on a bench, or almost anywhere. You will be using it with each sport in conjunction with the self-hypnosis exercises you will be doing.

A second form of relaxation is one that you can use while in the midst of play, and that is the one I will mention here. Have you noticed a professional tennis player (and many other athletes involved with sports where the pace of the game allows them to take a moment for such an exercise) stopping for a moment before starting to serve? The player may pause, the racket and ball held loosely, the player's eyes either closed or not fixed on the opponent. There seems to be a change in breathing for just a moment or two, and then the serve begins. The player is frequently controlling his or her breathing in order to have more control.

This simple breathing technique involves inhaling deeply, then holding your breath, and releasing it slowly over a count of about four beats. Often you will inhale through your nose, then exhale through your mouth. Inhale through your nose, and exhale through your mouth. Your entire body is limp while you focus only on your breathing. Inhale through your nose, and exhale through your mouth. Then open your eyes, and start the serve.

Such a breathing technique will calm your body in the midst of tension. It is not a substitute for reprogramming your subconscious through self-hypnosis, but it is a way to relax for a moment when you might otherwise becomes stiff.

Analyzing Your Attitude

Relaxing through breathing is important and can be done during the game. But the key to improving your tennis game is going to rest with your subconscious attitudes, which can easily be determined by analyzing the way you think about the game.

"I'm not an athlete, I'm a joke," Marilyn explained to me when we discussed her tennis game. "My mother always told me I run like a 'klutz.' She used to say that I could trip over my own feet just walking down the street. I look like a chicken with her head cut off when I run around the court. There's nothing anyone can do about that. I was a 'klutz' at five, I was a 'klutz' at fifteen, and I'm just as bad now that I'm an adult. You can't change me."

"It's too late for me to do well. I took up this game at forty because the doctor said I needed more exercise," said Frank, an overweight business executive attempting to get into better shape. "But everyone knows this is a kid's game. I'm too slow. I've lost too much strength. It's just physically impossible for an older man to take up tennis and do well."

Negative comments such as these may be similar to ones which you have made about your own game. Maybe you don't share Marilyn's bad image of herself or Frank's belief that age automatically cancels the ability to learn. Perhaps your beliefs about yourself reflect different negatives. Whatever the case, you are constantly rehashing the reasons why an action is not possible instead of recognizing that everyone can be better.

The reality is that each of us has different abilities, different strengths and weaknesses. Yet each weakness can be strengthened to some degree. Those so-called problem areas can be corrected through rethinking who you are and what you can do.

For example, take the case of the older athlete such as Frank. He was out of shape, overweight, and accustomed to a sedentary life. His activities had been mental. He was a business executive in a high-pressure job, yet the pressures taxed his mind, not his body. Thus he came to tennis stiff, with limited lung power, and with a subconscious fear that he would be viewed rather humorously by the younger players he saw on the courts.

Frank needed to be more realistic about who he was and where he was going. First, the fact that he was older actually gave him an edge over younger players as he learned the game. A young player may be more limber, able to rely on speed and power to dominate the court. But the older player has learned to think clearly and quickly under pressure. The older player can plan a strategy for a game so that he or she dominates the court. A serve may be weak, but if it is placed where you want it, you will know how to anticipate the location of the return and the way in which you will respond. Many an older player is able to stay in a relatively small area, sending the stronger, faster, younger opponent all over the court, destroying the supposed edge that younger opponent has.

Frank's muscles were not limber, but each day that he played he gained greater freedom of movement, more comfort with his body, and better control. He could spot the changes he was experiencing, changes which were for the better.

Weight loss was also accompanying Frank's game. It was a slow change, only a pound every week or two because he could not cut back that much on his diet, but he was getting lighter. Thus he could feel his body moving more easily since his heart was handling a lesser load of veins. Each pound of fat lost reflected a greatly reduced need for the body to work to maintain the flow of blood.

Thus Frank was benefiting greatly from his activity. He was always getting better. He simply needed to restructure his subconscious. Instead of saying, "I can't be as good as those kids who have been playing all their lives," he needed to be thinking, "Each hour on the court I am getting stronger, healthier, and more skilled." He needed to develop goals which were realistic and self-rewarding.

The same experience was true for Marilyn. She was developing eye-hand coordination. She was gaining speed. She was becoming a better player with each hour on the court. How she looked to a destructive mother who was constantly tearing her down, whether the mother realized that fact or not, was not important. Marilyn also needed to begin recognizing the changes and working to grow rather than returning to her negative attitude about herself.

The Failure of Positive Thinking

In the past, many athletes have relied upon a variation of the concept of positive thinking. Positive thinking is a method for change in which you constantly reinforce the best within you. Frank might jump out of bed each morning, look in the mirror, and say, "You may be over forty, but you've got the body and the brains to be the best there is. Today you're going to conquer those tennis courts. You're going to be a tiger out there who whips every opponent 6–0, 6–0, 6–0. You're going to play the best game of your life."

Theoretically, the constant reinforcement of these positive statements will change your abilities for the better. You will become what you wish to become, turning yourself into a winner.

The problem with positive thinking is that it requires constant repetition, and most people are not going to be able to sustain that. For example, suppose Frank stays up late Friday night. He works at the office overtime, then meets his wife for a drink. They go out to dinner, go dancing, and drink a little more than intended. Finally, about 1 A.M. they get home and go to bed, Frank setting his alarm for 7 A.M. because he has an early tennis game.

The alarm goes off, Frank groggily thrashing his hand in the general direction of the sound until he either turns off the alarm or accidentally smashes the clock. Then he sits up in bed, discovers he is slightly hung over, lies back down, and rolls off the bed onto the floor. There he rests for a moment before rising to his knees and making his way to the bathroom.

Finally he reaches the sink, pulling himself erect and staring into the mirror. He needs a shave, his hair is unkempt, there are bags under his eyes, and his breath is foul enough to melt the glass. As usual, he uses his positive-thinking approach to mumble to himself, "You may be over forty, but you've got the body and the brains to be the best there is." Then his subconscious mind says, "Who are you trying to kid? You've got a hangover, your knees are ready to buckle, and you look terrible. There are better-looking corpses in funeral homes before the mortician retouches their faces. You used to be able to dance all night and play all day, but now you look as though you're going to drop any second. Face it, Frank, you're not as young as you used to be. Looking at you, I'm not certain you were ever as young as you used to be. You think you're going to do well on the tennis court? You'll be lucky if you don't collapse in the middle of the first serve. Go back to bed with your wife. Maybe with a few days' rest, you'll at least look human."

Positive thinking has just been destroyed by the negative subconscious. Certainly Frank looked and felt terrible. Everyone does when they overdo it. He would be in the same shape if he was twenty, but he does not think about that fact. Positive thinking simply does not work when someone feels terrible, and everyone feels terrible at various times throughout the year. Even worse, once your positive-thinking approach is shattered by the subconscious attitudes, it is extremely difficult to regain it.

The Use of Self-Hypnosis

The way to reprogram your subconscious is through self-hypnosis. You will utilize positive images, each being realistic in what you are suggesting to yourself. You will set attainable goals with each practice session, and you will look for gradual change, not instant success, over time. Frank, at best, is not going to play tennis well on a Saturday when he has had five hours sleep and has a mild hangover. No one is going to play his or her best under such conditions. Positive thinking will tell him he should play well if he believes he can play well, a myth shattered by the physical realities. Self-hypnosis will help Frank understand that it does not matter how well he plays that Saturday. Over time, he is doing better, playing with greater skill and accomplishment. One bad game or even several bad games will not matter because his average progress is in a positive direction.

Planning Your Hypnosis Session

You do not want to try to change your abilities instantly. There are many areas on which you will want to concentrate, and these should be taken separately. Self-hypnosis works better the more you practice it. At first the benefits may seem minimal. The changes will be slight, and you might assume that they are the natural changes which come from regular play.

Then, as you use self-hypnosis each day for perhaps fifteen minutes, you will find that you are improving much more rapidly. You go under more easily, are able to remain under more deeply, and the suggestions you make to yourself are converted into progress that is recognizable almost at once. Thus you should start with the most important single change you wish to make in yourself, work on that for several days, then begin adding others as you see the changes taking place.

In the case of tennis, there are several points of concern. The player concerned with the dynamics of the game usually wishes to improve the serve, the backhand, and perhaps the timing of movement when going for a return. Such an individual may also want to think out strategy for the court, improving the ability to play according to a flexible plan which takes advantage of the court surface, the weather conditions, and the skill of the opponent.

For example, if your opponent has trouble with his backhand, you know that you want to place the ball in such a position that the backhand may have to be used. If the wind is strong, you will want to concentrate on power so that you have control. An advanced player may also place a slight spin on the ball so that it bounces oddly, the extra wind moving it faster away from your opponent in an unexpected direction caused by that spin. Or you may plan to strike the balls so that they consistently go to the far ends of the court, then suddenly lob one just over the net, forcing your opponent to have to rush forward unexpectedly.

Attitude changes are best planned with goals. "Over the next year, I am going to improve my serve so that I have more power and control. Each time I get the ball over the net on the first try, I will mentally award myself ten points. Each time I improve the smoothness of my serve and make it slightly more powerful, I will award myself five points." (The number of points you award yourself should be in direct proportion to the difficulty you find with that part of the game. Some players may have all the point scores the same. Others may vary them.) "Each time I place the ball so close to the line that my opponent fails to return my service, I will award myself fifteen points. And by the end of one year, I am going to have my serve improved to the point that I am awarding myself an average of twenty points each time."

What does this mean? It means that the goal is to have slightly more control with form and placement. The goal is not to be able to beat this year's champion at Forest Hills. It is not to have a serve so powerful and controlled that no one can return it. The goal is to be better on the average than in the past. This is attainable by everyone, does not lead to frustration, and results in an ever stronger game.

Another goal might be to have a smoother, more accurate back-hand over time. Or to increase your stamina so that you have as much energy at the end of a set as you had when you started. Instead of feeling competitive, you are working to be the best of which you are capable each day. Games that do not go your way do not matter because you are looking at the average. Games that do go your way simply reinforce your actions. Your subconscious mind stops tearing you down as you slowly improve your abilities.

You should also use self-hypnosis to give yourself positive rein-forcement for your actions. You will want to reward yourself for what you are doing so that you feel good about the progress you are making.

For example, Frank's subconscious reprogramming would include such positive statements as "I am taking better care of my body than I have in the past. I feel happier, healthier, and more alive after I play a game of tennis. I am mentally more alert. I am physically stronger. I like the way I am taking care of myself."

These statements are meant to reinforce Frank's actions with-out being destructive. He is not telling himself that he is going to be

Superman. He is letting his subconscious remind him that he feels better for exercising than he feels when he fails to exercise. Winning the game does not matter. His skill on the court does not matter. What matters is that he is playing.

Frank would make the reinforcement of the health and pleasure benefits of tennis his first priority. He has taken up the game for his health, and so he must reward the effort to play after so many years of sedentary life.

Next, Frank would work on whatever aspects of his game he feels are important. He might start with strategy since his mental alertness and ability to think clearly under pressure give him the greatest edge over younger, perhaps stronger, opponents. Then he would progress to other aspects of his game, such as the serve.

Marilyn's problem is somewhat different. She has a poor self-image on the court. She was raised to believe that she looks uncoordinated when she moves, and this has always hurt her.

Positive thinking, for Marilyn, might involve her repeating something such as "I am a beautiful woman. I am vibrant and exciting. I move with the grace of a professional fashion model." Unfortunately, her subconscious would constantly be saying: "Who do you think you are kidding? You walk like a one-legged duck. And beautiful? Maybe you have great hair, but it's too bad you can't do something about your nose. And those lines at your eyes. They look cute now, but give them a few years and you're going to need concrete to smooth them over."

With self-hypnosis, Marilyn's attitude toward herself was changed through suggestions to which she could relate. "Each time I play tennis, I am moving about the court with greater ease. My movements are becoming smoother, more graceful, and better coordinated."

In order to counter the negative thoughts about her appearance, Marilyn will use the positive imagery of "As I play tennis, my body is becoming more shapely. The activity is helping tone my skin. My complexion is becoming healthier in the sunlight, and I feel better about myself than ever before."

Notice that these suggestions cannot be destroyed by negative thought patterns. Marilyn easily can accept the idea of gradual change. She only will reject a positive statement which she feels is untrue. Perhaps she still thinks of herself as moving like a one-legged duck, but this time the "duck" is becoming more coordinated. She is better than she was. This may be only a slight change, but it is an improvement which she can accept. She is not ready to look upon herself with the objectivity others may have because she is still reacting to the hurt of her childhood ridicule. But she can feel better about herself, and it is this slight change which she constantly reinforces.

Eventually Frank will simply enjoy tennis and his healthier body without focusing on his age or what someone else can do. Eventually Marilyn will think of herself as a healthy, happy woman, as attractive a anyone else. But for now, the changes are coming through the use of suggestions which are both positive and realistic for their existing attitudes. And it is this same approach which you must use to improve your own skills on the courts.

What concerns you most when you play tennis? Is it winning? Then you might suggest to yourself, "I am going to enjoy my tennis game. I am going to be relaxed, alert, and play as effectively as I can today. I am going to take pleasure in my time on the courts." You will not try to dominate your opponent or try to reinforce winning because you are not always going to win. You may come up against a better player or have unfavorable weather conditions. You might accidentally hurt yourself or be unusually tired. Winning is a matter of luck, and luck has been said to be the experience which occurs when preparedness meets opportunity. Should you reinforce only the act of winning, you always will be working against any pleasure, and you frequently will be disappointed.

Your first job is to learn to enjoy tennis for the activity and the pleasure of the game. Then, like Frank, you will begin working on individual aspects of your game. Learning to relax, have fun, and gradually improve your skills will eventually translate into a winning game as well. But that winning game must not be your sole goal, as that is destructive to you, not constructive.

Is your goal to have a better serve, backhand, or some other technical improvement? Then you will want to improve slowly, rewarding yourself each time.

How long do you play tennis? Is this a seasonal sport for you? Then your reinforcement should be for the three to six months which might constitute that season. Do you play all year round? Then your goal should be for either the year or a portion of the year.

In Frank's case, he belonged to a tennis club with both indoor and outdoor courts. He spent the first month reinforcing the positive aspects of play. He came to look forward to his time on the courts, enjoying the increased stamina, improved health, and slowly decreasing potbelly. Then he took the next three months to make his primary suggestion the improvement of his serve. He still reinforced the pleasure of the tennis game, but he mainly worked on the technical aspect of his game. Another two months were spent on his backhand, the rest of the year concentrating on relaxation and eye-hand coordination to smooth out his forehand returns.

The length of time you work at your problems does not matter. Some people find that they have the changes they seek in a matter of days. Others take weeks. But all the suggestions eventually result in the desired improvements.

The Use of Visualization

The positive-reinforcement method for changing your subconscious will be accompanied by visual exercises. You will want to study the techniques you feel should be changed, either observing someone who does it well or remembering how you felt when everything fell into place.

For example, suppose you wish to improve your serve. You never have been able to serve effectively. Your timing and movement have always been wrong, and you have, in effect, been practicing poor technique. In this case, study the serve of someone whom you admire. This might be an instructor, another player, or a professional you have only seen on television. Watch their quality serves, and remember how they were accomplished. Then, while under self-hypnosis, you will remember this quality serve, placing yourself in the image so that you see yourself making the same movements that the player had made. Over and over again you will visualize yourself serving in the exact same way that the skilled player served. Then, when you are on the court, you will find that your body is beginning to imitate those skilled movements. You are developing the same serving ability as the player who serves as your inspiration.

If you have occasionally completed a perfect serve, though not nearly often enough for you to be comfortable with your game, think back to how you felt the time the serve was right. Think of how relaxed you were, the way your body was positioned, the sensation within your muscles, and the movement of your hand, arm, and racket. Relive this experience again and again under self-hypnosis. Think about how you are going to serve this way the next time you play tennis. Constantly reinforce this sensation, even to the point of mentally going through that serve under self-hypnosis before you leave for your game. The subconscious change you will have created will result in your increasing ability to match that perfect serve each time you play.

Practicing Hypnosis

First enter a state of self-hypnosis as described in Chapter 3. You will be relaxed, your mind focused only on what you want to change.

Now begin saying to yourself those positive messages which you need for change. Often this means starting with a statement such as:

"Each time I step on the tennis court, I will feel more and more relaxed. I will be alert, enjoying the challenge I am facing. In the past I may have felt competitive or frightened by an opponent, but now I am going to take pleasure in the game. Where once I felt I had to win, now I will find myself playing my best, comfortable in my abilities and my enjoyment of the game."

In order to change your serve, your backhand, or some other technical aspect of the game, you will start by visualizing the technique you want to master. Remember that this either can be a technique you can remember accomplishing at some time in the past, or it can be a technique you saw someone else achieve, such as when watching a professional match. If it is a technique you once achieved, try to visualize exactly what you did at that time. Try to remember your body's positions, the way your muscles felt, the direction of the ball, and all other aspects. This is often easiest to achieve with a serve you are trying to perfect.

If you are using another player as your role model, work from your memory of how the player handled the ball. Then picture yourself serving, returning the ball, etc. in the same manner. Visualize yourself as having this skill.

At the same time you are working on your visualization, say to yourself:

"Each time I serve, my body is going to be properly balanced, my swing complete, and the quality of my serve steadily improving. I will be developing more power, more control, and a more flowing movement, just as I am visualizing right now."

With the backhand, you might say to yourself:

"I am going to be moving into position for my backhand so that I am comfortable when the ball reaches me. I will be relaxed, my racket in position, my swing firm, hard, and controlled. I will place the ball where I am aiming just as I am visualizing right now."

You can make each technical change you need to make in this manner. Remember that all the statements you make to yourself must be positive ones. These will reinforce your visualization.

At this point you may be a little concerned about the visualization process. Many people are unable to fantasize. They are not able to visualize their body making a perfect swing, nor can they see themselves making the moves done by a professional.

Should this inability to visualize be a problem for you, there is a simple alternative. Think through the techniques you have been taught for a perfect serve, perfect backhand, or whatever other concern you have. Go through the steps, and tell yourself that each time you are playing, you will take those steps so that your movements are exactly as they should be. This will eliminate the pressures of trying to visualize and have the same positive results on the subconscious.

Practice, Practice, Practice

The subconscious mind is the key to your success, but it is not an alternative to practice. Your physical body will respond to your subconscious conditioning so long as your physical body is in shape. You cannot read a book on tennis, use self-hypnosis to train your subconscious mind to perfection, then step on the court for the first time in your life and expect to be a champion. However, if you practice regularly and combine that physical conditioning with the mental reinforcement, you will improve your game faster and to a greater degree than you ever thought possible.

Bowling

6

Bowling is one of the most psychologically difficult of all games you can play. The basic concept, rolling the ball down the alley toward the pocket in the pins, is fairly simple. It is a game which takes little power and thus can be enjoyed by both children and adults. Speed, strength, and other factors which may affect competition in other sports count for very little in bowling. Yet the ease of the game is countered by some unique stress factors.

"It's my friends," said Lynne, a league bowler with a ninety average. "I know they don't care how bad I am, or they wouldn't let me keep playing. But every time I start to roll the ball, I think about how I can't disappoint them. I know they're counting on me. I know they are hoping lightning will strike, and I'll do better. As I approach my mark, I keep telling myself, 'I'm not going to get a gutter ball. I'm not going to get a gutter ball.' But half the time I blow it, and I get that gutter ball, or I just knock over a few pins. They tell me they don't mind, but I do, and I think they'd be much happier having me on some other league or getting a better score at least once in a while."

"I'm all right with my first ball," said Greg, a beginning bowler who has been taking lessons for three months as a favor to his wife. She is the personnel director of a large manufacturing plant and has been bowling since elementary school. She knew Greg would never be up to her professional caliber, but she thought it would be fun if he took lessons so they could join a league together. "I feel the pressure when I have to roll a second time. If I have a split, I invariably go right between the pins. If I have to hit a side pin in order to knock everything down, I usually clip it so that only one goes. I know my wife probably doesn't care, but I want to impress her, and then I keep throwing away my second ball."

The reality of bowling is that the concept is simple but the actual game does have potential problem areas. For example, the way in which your thumb is pointed when you release the ball will determine where that ball ends up. A slight twisting away from the line the ball should follow, a twisting so minimal that you do not notice it as the ball rolls the first few feet down the alley, will result in a ball which cannot get a strike for you. That ball may clip only a few pins on the side or roll into the gutter.

Your psychological attitude as you approach your mark will also work for or against you. If you are constantly thinking about the gutter ball, that is how you will subconsciously turn your finger so that the ball ends in the gutter. The same is true when you are woried about making a 7–10 split or some other combination with your second ball. Your concern about a mistake will usually result in your making the mistake.

Remember how in Chapter 5 you learned that your body responds exactly as your subconscious suggests? This is true with every sport and especially with bowling, where the physical difference can be slight. Fortunately, the changes you are seeking are often much easier to make, again so long as you combine practice with your mental exercises and physical activity in the bowling alley.

Determining Your Problems

There are usually several areas which concern bowlers. The first is adjusting to the stress of standing alone at the alley, getting ready to roll the ball. The anxiety this creates can be identical to that experienced by a concert pianist, a comedian, or any other performer about to appear in a solo on the stage. You are alone, all eyes on you and the action you are about to take. You know that these people are looking to you to help the team score if you are bowling in a league. If you are just bowling with a friend, there may be a sense that the person is going to judge you based on how you roll the ball.

Intellectually, you know that your fears are unfounded. You are among friends, and the ball you roll down the alley is not going to radically change the world in which you live. Bowling is not a reflection upon life. There are no earthshaking events which will be won or lost on the roll of that ball. Winning or losing a game or tournament does not matter on any cosmic scale, or even to other friends and coworkers who are not in the alley that night.

The same situation is true when you are having a casual game with a friend. Neither the friend nor the people in the surrounding alleys are concerned with how you bowl. Naturally, if you are the type whose ball is hurled with such force that it bounces into the next alley, someone is certain to notice, but that is an unusual experience. Usually they care no more than you do, and I suspect that you are highly unlikely to watch the other lanes in case someone makes a mistake.

Continuing with objective reasoning, how many times have you stood in a bowling alley and seen a group of spectators march solemnly from lane to lane, watching the balls roll down the alleys? This group of reverse cheerleaders anxiously awaits the first mistake, at which time they chorus: "Gutter ball! Gutter ball! Dum-dum rolled a gutter ball!" Or "7–10 split! 7–10 split! Butterfingers didn't make the 7–10 split!"

Such events never take place. If people like that did exist, the owner of the bowling alley would throw them off the premises immediately. The owner wants your experience in the alley to be enjoyable. Such pressures would not be tolerated. Yet our anxieties do not reflect reality. The chorus may not exist for everyone else, but when we make a mistake, we tend to cringe, hearing this group of mythological harpies in our minds. No one else does and no one else cares. We simply fall victim to our own anxieties.

The fact that we have this anxiety at times means that this is one problem area we need to change. It is not a problem in the physical reality of our friends and surroundings. It is a problem with our subconscious, so this is one area we will have to consider when developing a self-hypnosis program for change.

The second major difficulty is with the way in which you are technically playing the game. You are making no mistakes when you play. That ball is going exactly where you are sending it. You are thinking "gutter ball" and subconsciously twisting your hand just enough so that is where the ball is aimed when you release it. You will need to restructure your subconscious mind for a more positive direction. You will be able to insure that whatever way you should be holding the ball will be the way in which you do hold it.

A third difficulty is muscle fatigue, which makes controlling the ball harder than when you are fresh. This fatigue may set in after two or three games, or it may come later. Sometimes it is the result of your being inexperienced with bowling. You are not used to holding the weight of the bowling ball. You are not accustomed to the motions your hand, wrist, arm, and shoulder must make. You become fatigued simply because you are not yet accustomed to the game. With time, your muscles will become more developed.

The other reason for fatigue is psychological, as you saw in the earlier chapters of this book. You use the tiredness as an excuse for doing poorly. The anxiety you have generated concerning your bowling makes you become tired as an escape mechanism. You are given an excuse to have difficulty, an excuse which actually prevents you from doing the best of which you are capable. Or you are given an excuse to stop bowling. The muscle weakness means you need to rest for a while and will have to stop playing. Both excuses seem valid but are actually created through your emotions toward bowling.

Using Self-Hypnosis to Correct Problems

The first step with any self-hypnosis program is to learn to relax. You want to eliminate any anxiety you have when you are bowling.

Chapter 3 offers suggestions for relaxing your body as you enter self-hypnosis. These should be practiced repeatedly before going on to make corrections in your game.

Next consider the problem of anxiety. Becoming an expert bowler will take time and practice, not just self-hypnosis, though many professionals use self-hypnosis as an important part of their training program. Thus you are not going to show instant improvement so dramatic that you take your team from last place to first.

Bowling averages also are not going to rise that much if you are starting the self-hypnosis techniques well into the season. Each game score is added together, then the total score is divided by the number of games you have played in order to find your average. If you have played ten games and earned a score of 60 per game, and then you suddenly hit 90 on your next game, that is a wonderful improvement. You are bowling 50 percent better than in the past and should be very proud of yourself. But as to your average score, you were averaging 60 (ten games times sixty pins per game for a total of 600 points. Divide the total points by the number of games and you have 60 average) and now, with that remarkable improvement of thirty pins on your eleventh game, your average is only 62.7 (690 points for the eleven games. You are dividing eleven into 690 for the average score).

What does this mean? Your self-hypnosis technique may greatly improve the way you bowl, but you must be realistic about your seasonal average. Your improved scores are compensating for the earlier low scores. Thus you should realistically expect an average to rise by no more than ten to a maximum of twenty pins in a season. Naturally, the sooner you start this technique, combining it with individual practice separate from the team play, the greater the average change you will have. But most people turn to this approach when they have been bowling for a while and are dissatisfied. This means that even with dramatic improvement for each game, you must accept the reality that the average score change will be between ten and twenty pins for the season. Thus such a change is a realistic goal.

In order to achieve this goal, you will be giving yourself positive suggestions while in hypnosis. Some of these will be reinforcing the correct way to hold your body while you bowl. Others will be positive suggestions concerning your average score.

It is important that you not try to change each and every game that you bowl. You must not suggest to yourself that each ball you roll will be a strike or that each game you roll will be a perfect one. The individual games do not matter, since you are going to vary in your ability due to genuine tiredness, the normal highs and lows everyone experiences at different times, the oddities of a particular lane, and other factors. You may even have an occasional off night where nothing seems to go right, just as happens with top professionals. So long as you are looking for the average change throughout a season and not an instant change in any given night, you will not become discouraged.

I mentioned positive thinking in the previous chapter, and the concern I have about such methods applies here. Suppose you use a form of positive thinking, constantly saying to yourself, "Tonight I am going to bowl a perfect 300 game. I feel good. I feel strong. I am capable of making a strike each time I approach my mark. I am a winner, and I am going to make strike after strike tonight."

Such statements are excellent positive-thinking concepts. You are viewing yourself as a winner. You are demanding perfection from yourself. You are thinking positively, determined to succeed, nothing to stop you. Unfortunately, you are also creating so rigid a concept that failure does not seem possible, yet the reality is that if you have never broken 100 as a bowler, the idea of instantly achieving a 300 game is unlikely.

Then you step to the alley. All eyes are upon you, yet you are supremely self-confident because you have been using your positive thinking. You approach your mark, release the ball, and watch it roll almost flawlessly down the alley. "Almost" is the critical word, though. The ball is off ever so slightly, and you have a spare.

"I'm no good!" your subconscious mind suddenly shouts. "I used positive thinking to bowl a 300 game and look at me, I get a spare the first time up and there goes my game. I'm a rotten bowler, and I might as well be honest with myself about that fact."

The reality might be quite different. The reality might be that this is the best you have ever accomplished when approaching your first time with the ball. You may always have knocked down just two or three pins the first time you play in any game, yet tonight you rolled a spare. Unfortunately, instead of taking pride in your unusual accomplishment, you feel helpless because the strike "positive thinking" told you would be obtained proved to be a spare instead.

The use of self-hypnosis does not rely upon the magic of one event. You are not going to suggest that you will be rolling perfect games right from the start. Instead you are reprogramming yourself for an improved average over time. You might have a bad game or even a bad night. Your score may actually go down slightly for some games, yet this will never be a concern for you. Over time, the self-hypnosis techniques will make you a better bowler. You are going to improve your average every season that you are using these methods. Remember that even the top money-making professionals have off nights, but they know that, over time, they will be extremely successful.

Return to Chapter 3, and study the self-hypnosis techniques described in that chapter. Next begin practicing, starting with suggestions to ease the anxiety which can occur when bowling. Make each suggestion positive and related to problems you are having.

For example, suppose you are nervous about people watching you when you bowl. Among the suggestions you might make to yourself are:

"Each time I start to bowl, I will feel relaxed and happy. I will remember that I am with friends. I will enjoy the sharing of the evening. I will look forward to taking my turn because it makes me feel a part of the group."

"Going bowling brings me peace of mind. Being with friends in the bowling alley is an enjoyable experience. I like taking my turn. I enjoy rolling the ball and seeing how well I can do each time. I know my friends support my efforts and are proud that I am doing the best I can each time, no matter what my score for that ball."

These suggestions are all positive. They all reinforce the end of that performance anxiety you have been experiencing.

Some of the bowlers who come to me for help have difficulty relaxing just with the positive suggestions I have provided here. (Always remember that the suggestions included in this book are not magic formulas. They are guides to show you one of several correct ways to use self-hypnosis. You may want to change to your own suggestions, using the approach I have shown only as a guide.) They may want to add suggestions to narrow their attention to the ball and the alley. For example, they may wish to add such suggestions as:

"The moment I pick up my ball, I will stop being strongly aware of my friends and the other people at the bowling alley. I will think only of how I am to approach my mark and release the ball. I will be oblivious to the people around me. The sounds of the other bowlers and spectators will be like soothing background music. The sounds will drift over and through me, though I will not pay attention to any of the words or the actions of others. The sounds will be soothing, relaxing, enabling me to play my best. I will not focus on the words or the movement all around. I will see only my alley and concentrate only on the release of the ball."

This second type of suggestion, and remember that it is only a guide you can modify for your own needs, further reduces anxiety by changing how you perceive your surroundings. Some bowlers are constantly listening to conversations all around them, the sounds of other balls going down other alleys, the happy chatter of spectators, and all the other stimuli which exist in such surroundings. They have trouble focusing on the task at hand—rolling that ball down the alley as effectively as possible.

You will notice that none of these suggestions has to do with improving your technical skills as a bowler. They are simply meant to help you relax and stop being influenced by the people and sounds all around you. Once you have achieved this end, it is time to add suggestions related to your technical skills.

Relieving Improper Technique

There are two ways to alter improper technique for every sport. One approach is visualization, the utilization of your imagination to actually see a difference within your mind. Many people are able to visualize, and this is the way they should plan their self-hypnosis.

There are others who cannot visualize. They will be handling their changes by reviewing proper technique while in self-hypnosis. They will take each step of a correct approach, ball-handling position, and release, thinking about it in their minds, planning to duplicate this knowledge on the alley.

Start by considering what it is that you wish to change about your bowling. Is it your approach? The way you hold the ball? The way you release your ball? There might be one change you wish to make or several.

Next think about how to make that change. Have you ever had a perfect strike where you could sense every muscle, every hand position, your body balance, and all other factors were exactly as they should be? Try to remember what you did and all the physical sensations you experienced at that time. Now imagine yourself making those same moves. Picture yourself in the bowling alley among the friends with whom you normally bowl. Mentally pick up the ball and begin your approach. Find the pocket and your spot, releasing the ball just as you did when you had that strike. Try to feel all your body positions, perhaps picturing yourself making that strike in much the manner as you might watch some other player. Then mentally observe the ball rolling down your imaginary alley, hitting the pins perfectly, knocking them all down.

Naturally you may not remember such a time. Perhaps you have never had a strike. Or perhaps you have had strikes but have no idea how you accomplished this act. Under such circumstances, visualize some other bowler making all the right moves. This might be an instructor you have had. It might be a fellow player whose skill is currently well in advance of your own. Or it might be a professional bowler you have watched on television. Whatever the case, you will want to picture this individual going through all the proper steps.

Next change that image so that you see yourself making all those correct moves. Now you are the bowler you have admired. You have transposed his or her body with your own. You are watching yourself do everything right and imagining how you will look in your next games.

Enhance this visualization with positive suggestions. Tell yourself how you will hold the ball. Tell yourself how you will be positioned and how your body will feel as the ball is released. Tell yourself that with this improved technique, your average score is going to increase by a minimum of ten pins in the course of the season. Tell yourself how good it will feel to make every move a correct one so that you have more control, more power, and more accuracy than ever before.

The same basic situation holds true if you are one of the many individuals who can not fantasize and visualize. Instead of trying to see yourself, review the steps for a perfect strike. Tell yourself how you will duplicate these steps, from the way you hold the ball to the position of your thumb as the ball is released from your hand. Enhance these statements with other positive means of reinforcement, such as:

"I will feel most comfortable as I approach my spot and release the ball. I will feel confident, strong, and relaxed as I follow these techniques. I will be more accurate than ever before. I will be improving my technique and gradually raising my average score throughout the coming weeks."

Every statement should be positive. Every statement should avoid any "magical" concepts such as: "I will bowl at least five strikes a game" or "I will bowl 175 or better tonight." Self-hypnosis is not a crutch. It is a proven method for altering the subconscious mind, that portion of your mind which controls so many of your physical actions when you are participating in any athletic event.

Establishing a System of Rewards

You can enhance your subconscious reprogramming by giving yourself rewards for your achievements. One easy method is to give yourself a set number of points for each improvement. For example, you might give yourself one point for each five points of improvement in a game. This is an improvement over your normal score, so that if you are a bowler who has been averaging around 80, you gain a point for scoring 85, two points for scoring 90, and so forth. This does not require you to have a set number of strikes or spares. It is a reward for the average improvement in a game.

Another reward might come from reducing the number of gutter balls regardless of your final score. If you have been averaging eight gutter balls a game (I know, you might have far more as I used to do; this is just an example), you can reward yourself five points when you roll seven or less. Your score may not improve, but obviously you are beginning to use better technique because the ball is rolling properly.

Keeping a score sheet of rewards will be much easier than trying to keep track of your average score changes from week to week. You may have an off night, which can be a little discouraging, even though you know that the self-hypnosis approach is always making your growing average much better. Yet even on an off night, you may be able to give yourself five points because of the decrease in gutter balls, if that is one of your concerns. Even if it is truly an off night, one of those times when the ball will never go where you wish, you can still take comfort in the fact that, over time, you are getting better.

The techniques described in this chapter will work effectively for you. They have helped countless beginning and advanced bowlers over the years. Many professionals use self-hypnosis not only to achieve their consistently high scores but also to cope with the stress of being on the road and the tension of bowling for an audience.

Be certain to read the other chapters of this book as well because you will find suggestions for players of other sports which you may wish to adopt for bowling. Everyone is unique, and what works for one person in one sport may also be effective for quite a different sport. Thus you can gain from the experience of athletes in a number of fields even as you are improving your average bowling score faster and more effectively than you ever thought possible.

Running

7

For millions of Americans, athletic activity means the pleasures and the agonies of short- and long-distance running. Whether someone is an avid jogger or prefers the less jarring movement of a run, this seems to be the ideal exercise. A good pair of shoes is all that is needed, almost any clothing being appropriate. You can run through country fields and meadows, along major highways, or in the heart of urban activity. Stop by Manhattan's most expensive luxury hotels early in the morning, and you will find business executives taking the elevator to the street level so they can run from Broadway to Wall Street to Fifth Avenue. Midday running enthusiasts may prefer Central Park, going over on their lunch hour, then changing back into their business clothes before returning to their desks.

A trip into farm country anywhere in the Midwest will reward you with the sight of men and women racing across endless stretches of highways adjacent to the fields of wheat, corn, and other crops. And in California, running is frequently done along the beaches adjacent to the endless stretch of ocean.

Runners have numerous motivations from taking up their activity. For some it is just a simple way to stay in shape without going to any serious expense. Once you have a pair of running shoes, you can exercise anywhere, at any hour, without having to pay health club fees or buy balls, rackets, clubs, or anything else. You can run alone or with a group. Couples with a determined attitude of togetherness may maintain their closeness by having one person run while the other accompanies on a bicycle.

Other runners like a certain amount of competition. Sometimes this is self-competition involving a personal attempt to run faster, further, or meet some other internal goal. At other times they enjoy short fun runs of a few miles. Still others want to engage in long-distance marathons which may go twenty-six miles or more.

Runners may go out for from fifteen to thirty minutes a day, or they may train like top athletes, putting almost as much time on the road as they put in on their jobs. In fact, some runners become so obsessed with racing several hundred miles a week that they sacrifice family, friends, social life, and all other activities. A few doctors have even gone so far as to suggest that this extreme obsession is no different from the compulsion to starve to death which results in anorexia nervosa.

What Type of Runner Are You?

Success as a runner requires the right attitude toward running. Many people run for the fun of running. It has been learned that when you run, two biological changes occur. One is that the natural exposure to sunlight results in the formation of a natural tranquilizer. This is the result of a photobiology which converts sunlight into a natural form of Vitamin D, a form which brings peaceful relaxation.

Running is not essential for the photobiology to take place. A brisk walk or a jog will have the same results. In fact, almost any exercise enjoyed outdoors for at least thirty minutes a day can have this effect.

The second reaction is the creation of Beta-endorphins, the substance which produces the natural "high" that many long-distance runners and walkers experience each time they are out. Runners often talk about "breaking the wall" and "getting a second wind." What they really mean is that there is some point when they are running when they suddenly feel euphoric, stimulated, and full of enjoyment in what they are doing. They may have started to become tired just before this moment. They may have been somewhat winded and thinking of taking a rest. Then suddenly there is a physical and mental change which makes the runner feel as though he or she could continue on forever. It is at this point that the Beta-endorphins have been released.

There is also the stimulation which comes from the increased circulation of your blood. As you engage in any sport, your body's blood flow and the oxygen level of the brain improve. You may be a little tired when you start to run, then find yourself stimulated to a level where you can think and act more clearheadedly immediately afterward. Many people find that they are physically tired after running but mentally more alert and able to handle creative tasks with greater ease.

For all these reasons, you may be the type of runner who simply enjoys being in shape and feeling good. You may wish to move faster and be more relaxed. You may wish to try to increase the distance you can run so that you can enjoy noncompetitive "fun runs" where winning is not important.

You also might be a competitive individual who wants to go faster and/or further than in the past in order to compete in races. You may want to become faster as a sprinter, a miler, or a marathon runner. Your competition may be within your school or through a club to which you belong. Or you may be the type who likes to travel to various races around your state and elsewhere, competing with runners who may have traveled across the country or around the world. The participants in the New York and Boston marathons fall into these categories.

You might even be the obsessed type of runner who will sacrifice everything else of value in order to go more miles each day. This is an extreme reaction to a sport which ideally should provide pleasure. If these are your circumstance and you are reading this book, chances are that you want to make running fun again. You want to place it in perspective in your life so that you are not sacrificing loved ones, work, and quiet pleasures in the obsessive drive to go ever more miles each week.

Changing the Subconscious for Positive Ends

The first change you want to make is in your attitude toward running. You want your subconscious mind to recognize that running is enjoyable. It has positive results which should be the underlying reasons for your involvement with the sport. Every other goal you wish to achieve will be easier to reach with that basic thought process.

Relax yourself and place yourself in a state of self-hypnosis. This should be done at home and is separate from any conditioning you might do.

Once you are ready, begin telling yourself such positive statements as:

"I feel good about myself when I run." "I am relaxed when I start to run. I know my body will respond with power and speed because I am so comfortable and at ease. It doesn't matter whether I'm running alone or in competition. I always feel relaxed and happy when I begin my run." "Running makes me happy. When I start my run, I am happy I am getting such enjoyable exercise. When I complete my run, I am happy that I have made the effort. I feel relaxed, mentally alert, and better able to carry on with my day."

Obviously you can tailor the positive statements to fit your needs. One highly competitive runner told me, "Just before we start, I feel terrible. I have trouble breathing. I yawn a lot. I know I'm too tired to do well, and I often am slower getting started than I should be. I keep thinking that I might be sick, and if I'm sick, I shouldn't be running. It's all in my head. I know I'm just uneasy about the competition and, once I get started, I'm always fine. But it bothers me that I go through such a negative litany of problems each time I am on the starting line."

The runner who made these statements was no novice. She had been running since high school. She earned many trophies in college and had been competing in marathons for the past ten years. She has won numerous events and truly loves what she does. However, she also has had the type of love-hate relationship with getting started which resulted in her developing the reactions she described. For her, the answer was to make the following statements:

"I feel relaxed when I am going to compete. As I warm up, each breath I take comes easier to me. I feel increasingly alert. I feel happier and more relaxed as the competition draws near. My body is stimualted by the anticipation of the run, and I am happy to be running. I like myself. I like what I am doing. And I feel rested, alert, relaxed, and in control at the start." These phrases all helped her have a more positive mental attitude. They also specifically addressed her problems, always implying that her efforts would be easier. She never said that her breathing would be perfect because this might have led to an effort to consciously reject that suggestion. However, the suggestion that she would feel more comfortable with each breath was one she could easily handle.

Next visualize yourself as you are about to run. See yourself being relaxed, alert, your body ready for the run. Visualize yourself being happy, looking forward to either the exercise or the competition, depending upon whether or not you run alone.

Also visualize yourself at the end of the run. You might see yourself being flushed with the pleasure of what you have done. You will see yourself as still relaxed but feeling even better than before. You will imagine yourself either crossing the finish line or returning to your home, office, or school feeling awake, alert, and happy for having had experience.

Some runners also like to visualize themselves at the midway point in their run or at whatever stage they normally feel a little fatigued. They imagine how they look as they move gracefully, their legs traveling with muscles relaxed and power surging through their body. They see themselves breathing more and more comfortably, a smile on their face, as they go along sidewalks, parks, roadways, or countryside.

As mentioned earlier in this book, there will be some of you who cannot visualize or imagine how you will look in these circumstances. Should you be this type of individual, you will want to tell yourself how you feel. You can make positive statements about the pleasures you are gaining, describing how you will look, the smile on your face, and so forth.

This exercise is meant to change your subconscious attitudes. The more relaxed you are during your run, the happier you are with yourself and the actions you are taking, the faster you can go with greater safety. You will be less likely to be bothered by overwhelming fatigue. You will also not have that uncontrolled adrenalin surge which can tire you early in the competition.

A relaxed runner, especially in competition, will control the surge of adrenalin needed for a rapid finish. The tense runner may start to feel that adrenalin flow at the starting line, racing to a fast start which ends with fatigue, often before the person is halfway through the race. The ability to pace the run, planning a final burst of speed, is lost because of the early tension. Thus the reprogramming of the subconscious mind will help alleviate this problem.

Runners have a number of problems they face, depending upon the distance they run, the competition they face, and the reasons they are running. Many of these problems are based on a combination of myths and realities which have become intermingled in the minds of both runners and coaches. For example, everyone "knows" there is a limit to how fast the human body can run. The faster you go, the harder it is not to oxygenate the brain. There is a barrier you cannot break without collapsing into unconsciousness.

This great truth of maximum speed is based on the mythology of the times. I can remember when it was impossible for the human body to break the four-minute mile. No human could run that fast. Everyone knew this "fact," and runners seldom let themselves do more than approach it. Their subconscious minds had them slow down or become tired when their early pace was fast enough so that breaking this barrier might become a reality.

Suddenly a runner came along who had not heard that breaking the four-minute mile was "impossible." This runner not only accomplished the "impossible," he convinced others that they could achieve this feat.

Next came the new barriers. Three minutes, fifty-five seconds was the maximum a human could endure, was one theory. Then that time was reached, a second shaved, and a new barrier announced. Some runners believed this "wisdom." Others just ran to the best of their abilities, their subconscious minds telling them that anything was possible. They kept achieving what no one else had done, constantly shattering the "truism" once so steadfastly believed.

The reality is that no one knows just how fast someone can run or when a limit might be reached. People are so different from one another that it is also possible that there are individuals genetically different to just enough of a degree that what is "impossible" for one runner is a realistic goal for another. More important, the only way you are going to know this fact is to constantly push yourself to your current limits and then reach slightly beyond. The more you run, the easier running becomes. Your lungs develop stamina, your muscles become stronger, and you develop a more natural stride which enables your body to function more efficiently. There is no way to know what your limit might be, and there is a good chance that you will be improving your entire life, never encountering an "ultimate" barrier for yourself.

There may be circumstances when one runner seems to have an advantage over another. For example, if two runners are able to move their legs at exactly the same speed, a runner with longer legs will win the race. Often this leads a short runner to mentally accept the probability of losing when a tall competitor is in the same race. But the tall person may have greater limitations. The tall person may be working to capacity as he or she runs, while the shorter person may be growing ever faster and stronger. The short person may find that winning is easy, so long as the subconscious mind has not given up.

The reverse is also true. A tall runner may be subconsciously deciding that all the extra size and weight means that the shorter runner has an advantage. The shorter runner can move more quickly and thus will "always" be the winner. The taller runner does not bother to develop the full potential for speed, stamina, and positive attitude which could make the true difference in competition.

Using Self-Hypnosis for Speed

In order to increase your speed, you will want to place yourself into a state of self-hypnosis and begin making positive statements such as:

"There are no limits to how fast I can run. Each day that I run, I am increasing my average speed. There may be days when I run more efficiently than others, but gradually my running is becoming faster and faster" "I relax when I start to run. I keep my muscles relaxed, my body relaxed, my mind at ease. And as I feel myself relax, my stride becomes more efficient. My muscles power me more effectively. I run faster, easier, and more effectively than I have ever run before. As I gradually improve, I realize that there are no limits to my potential speed. I relax and run, my average speed getting ever faster."

Naturally, you will want to tailor the statements you make to your particular needs. At the same time you should start visualization techniques.

Have you ever run when you felt your body was responding perfectly? Maybe you were running alone and wished that you could have been competing with someone because you know that that day, you were unbeatable. How did you feel when you were running? Try to remember your stride, the relaxed effort your muscles were making as they propelled you across the ground, and the ease with which you were breathing. Mentally recreate that experience and tell yourself that this is the way you will regularly feel when you run. Do not say that you will always feel this way because everyone has good and bad times. Just remind yourself that these experiences will be yours with greater and greater frequency.

You can also visualize a runner you have seen whose efficiency and speed are greater than anything you have ever achieved. This might be someone you saw on television competing in an international event. Or it might be someone you watched at a track and field event, during a marathon, or even a race you were in.

Next, imagine this runner competing, only this time substitute your body for that of the superior runner. Now picture yourself in competition, doing what he or she had accomplished. It does not matter if your role model is a male or a female. The sex is not important, just the skill. Thus a man may visualize a highly successful woman runner, substituting his body for hers. Or a woman may visualize a highly successful male runner, mentally substituting her body for his. The techniques of running successfully are the same for both sexes, and you want to be the best runner imaginable.

Again, if you have trouble visualizing all this, talk yourself through the change you wish to make in your skill. Describe the difference in stride, the way the body is relaxed over distance, the point where there is a controlled burst of speed, and all the other details. Tell yourself that this is how you will be running, your speed greater than ever before.

You should also begin visualizing strategy if you are concerned with winning a race. Plan the way you are going to run, the start you will make, the way you will move through the pack of runners, and the way you will make your final burst of speed. Always concentrate on being better than you were in the past. Do not set a goal of beating a particular runner in a particular race because, if you do, you may find that he or she has an unusually good day. You are running faster than you have ever done before, but so is your competitor. You may have previsualized yourself passing this competitor at a particular turn, then found yourself unable to make this pass. The result can be extreme discouragement, where you stop pushing so hard. The conscious reality overcomes the subconscious programming, and you start to give up. Yet the reality may be that you were running better than before. You had made great improvement and, with better subconscious programming, you could have achieved more than ever before, even though you did come in second to this rival.

Always set yourself for improvement. With practice and a running strategy that does not require you to be "better than" anyone else, you will go faster and faster. You will begin to achieve what you once thought was impossible.

Correcting Other Problems

Many runners have minor problems that affect their performance. Sometimes this is becoming winded at a certain point in their run. At other times it is difficulty getting off to a fast start or a tensing of the muscles which occurrs regularly, perhaps when you are attempting to put on a burst of speed. Or it might be some other consistent problem you have noticed and not found a way to counter. Whenever the circumstances, you can correct them using the same techniques.

This time place yourself into a state of self-hypnosis, and concentrate on the problem area. Picture yourself running at whatever point trouble normally occurs. Then imagine yourself passing through the difficulty.

For example, if you routinely have trouble breathing a third of your way into your run, visualize yourself breathing with ever great ease at that point. Tell yourself, "The more I run, the easier my breathing becomes. I feel better and gain all the oxygen I need. Each stride helps me breathe with ever greater comfort."

Is your trouble getting off to a rapid start? Picture yourself achieving the start you desire as you say, "I am relaxed at the starting line. My muscles have only enough tension to allow for a smooth, extremely rapid takeoff. Each time I run, I can feel my starts becoming faster, stronger, and more comfortable."

Do your muscles seem to tense toward the end of the run? Again visualize your run as being increasingly comfortable. At the same time, say something to the effect of: "The more I run, the more my body relaxes. My muscles lose all stiffness. Movement becomes easier. I am relaxed, in full control of my body, enjoying the run and the competition. The faster I drive myself, the more relaxed my muscles feel. It is a pleasure to run. I am delighting in the experience."

You should follow this approach for every problem you face. Just adapt the visualization and suggestions for the specific concern you have.

Techniques for the Casual Runner

Most of the techniques described have been designed for the competitor. You may have no interest in competition, merely enjoying a solitary run several times a week as a means of keeping in shape. Yet even though you are not in competition, you still wish to be better than you have been in the past.

The techniques you will use are quite similar to those which improve a competing runner's skills. This time you are probably going to have only two main concerns, speed and distance. You either want to run longer than in the past or you want to cover the same ground in less time.

In order to run longer, you will not only have to build physical stamina, because the body requires development for long distance, you will also have to counter the mental barriers. Under self-hypnosis, you will want to suggest some positive ideas as: "The longer I run, the more relaxed I become. My breathing is easier with distance. I feel stronger, confident, and am enjoying my run as I go a little further than I have in the past." "Each day that I run, I am getting stronger, my stamina increasing. I am able to run a little further as the days pass. My average run is getting longer and longer."

Naturally, you can vary this for your needs. You can even set a goal for yourself. For example, suppose you always run to the base of a hill and back. You might suggest to yourself: "When I reach the hill I will feel stronger and have my breathing well controlled. I will want to run a little further, going part way up the hill before I start my return." Then, as you increase your distance, you can suggest to yourself that you go all the way to the top of the hill, perhaps eventually going to the other side before returning. Whatever your goal, you work toward it gradually.

In the case of speed, you will work on those factors which will make a difference. You can suggest to yourself that your muscles are relaxed, that your breathing is controlled, and that you feel better as you run faster. If there are points where your pace slows, you might suggest that your stride will remain consistent or become more rapid. Just maintaining an average stride can increase your speed if you had been slowing for part of the distance.

You also can set goals for yourself. If you have been going to a certain spot and back, you might pick a location slightly further down the road and suggest that you will reach that spot and return in the same time as you did the shorter distance.

No matter what approach you use, make certain that it is gradual. Your body is far stronger than you realize, and this translates into its ability to run faster almost immediately. However, by having yourself slowly increase your speed, you will not find a negative reward when you have a day when you are tired and not quite as effective as a runner. Rather than becoming discouraged, you will be able to look with pride at the gradual change for the better which you are experiencing.

Whether you are running for fun or competition, the steps in this chapter will greatly improve your abilities. Remember to plan your program carefully so you are looking at average changes, then combine this with regular exercise. Success is a combination of body and mind, and you must not neglect either one.

Boxing and the martial arts

8

There was a time when boxing was the sport of ghetto hopefuls anxious to rise above poverty in the only way available to them and martial arts could be learned only in the Orient. However, as the popularity of Golden Gloves training spread to middle America, boxing clubs became fashionable. Then such martial arts training as Tae Kwon Do became available in suburban shopping malls, and these activities have attracted thousands.

Even with its new-found respectability, boxing was considered dangerous. However, this changed when children and young adults took to using helmets to avoid head damage, thus eliminating some of the well-grounded fears about such training. They learned to box for the love of the sport and the body building that results, seldom having any thought of a professional career.

Martial arts training has far fewer inherent dangers. Such training now attracts everyone from doctors and lawyers to small children who are also studying piano, ballet, and similar pursuits.

If you are interested in either of these forms of self-defense, there is a good chance that your subconscious programming has been somewhat negative. Boxing especially is filled with myths that have become feared "truisms" over the years. Talk with any sports fan, and you will learn that a boxer must (choose one or more): "Have that killer instinct." "Be black." "Be white." "Be German." "Be [add your own color, creed, and nationality as you see fit]." "Have massive arms." "Have short arms." "Be a power puncher." "Have the grace of a dancer." "Move like a Sherman tank." "Delight in drawing blood." "Be a gentleman." "Train under [Big Louie, Knuckles Bradshaw, Rocky, etc.]." "Train alone." "Be born with *it*." "Acquire *it* with training." And on and on and on . . .

Professional boxers are even worse than amateurs when it comes to superstitions, their reactions to hype, and other factors. The prefight hype is filled with rhetoric. "I am the greatest." "He is old, he is paunchy, but he can take a punch, and he has heart that no younger opponent can handle." "He is the '*no mas*' fighter." "You can throw away the record book on this one. Tough Tommy Tillinghurst has been KO'd during the last thirty-seven fights, but this is a grudge match with his eighty-seven-year-old grandmother in the audience. You can throw away the record books on this one because Tough Tommy has promised the old lady he is going to smash in the face of the champion, and the champion knows that his title is at stake."

Then there are the superstitions. "I can win only when I have three raw eggs and a glass of orange juice for breakfast." "I have to train at Caesar's Palace in Las Vegas between 7:07 P.M. and midnight." "I must have the gloves with my lucky brass knuckles in them." Take away the champion's rubber ducky, and he is likely to think that he cannot win the match.

Certainly the hype is silly, but the fighters often come to believe it. Two grown men, superb physical specimens, natural athletes who have trained for months suddenly find themselves cowering in fear because they each have heard that the other is going to win the "battle of the century [or year, or month, week, day, or hours]." Then they begin boxing, each man covering up as much as possible, their blows tentative, their actions a model of restraint. Sometimes this lasts for fifteen rounds, one of the fighters winning on points and the audience disgusted by the lack of skill shown by both men. At other times one of them lands a solid punch. The opponent goes down or is obviously hurt. The first boxer suddenly realizes that perhaps he can win.The man he feared is not made of impregnable concrete. He begins boxing in earnest while his opponent is even more nervous and eventually loses.

There also have been occasions when both boxers break through the defenses of the opponent. They each realize that their fears were groundless, and they begin boxing like the true professionals they have trained to be. The fight becomes an excellent example of the art of boxing, and the crowd delights in it. Yet the change still occurs only after they have first yielded to the myths of the prefight hype.

What does all this mean to you? It means that your abilities as a boxer are determined, in large measure, by your mental attitude. Whether you enjoy this sport for fun and body building or seriously want to compete in the amateur or professional ring, taking control of your subconscious mind is the key to success.

Martial Arts Myths

The martial arts have become among the most popular forms of exercise available in the United States. They combine all the movements of classical ballet with training that develops both the mind and body to handle such violence on the street. The various forms come from Korea, Japan, Okinawa, and other locations. Some are taught as exercises, some are taught as sports,and some are taught as a combination of physical fitness and self-defense. A few forms of karate encourage the toughening of the hands, though such extremely popular variations such as Tae Kwon Do (Korean karate) use the body naturally so that even someone who is aged or has arthritis can master them.

The myths of martial arts often evolve from motion pictures and television shows. For example, the Japanese have released a series of action adventure films involving karate, kung fu, and other martial arts. The speed and dexterity of the experts shown seem to imply that the average person can never have such skill. Yet the reality is that the films have their fight scenes speeded up in many instances and, in other cases, the fighting shown is choreographed. The moves made, if actually made on the streets, would not be safe against an opponent.

For example, many people over thirty have hestitated to take up the martial arts even though they are interested in them because they fear that they will not be able to do all the leaping moves they have seen. Yet the reality is that the leaping moves, though powerful and dramatic, are exercises. They help to train and develop the body. They are especially useful for the young who have the stretch and agility, because they can get into shape quickly and retain that shape into old age if they keep practicing. But the older student is likely to never be able to make some of those moves, and this fact does not matter. The American Tae Kwon Do Association (with 500 schools and over 100,000 members at this writing), for example, trains the severely handicapped and the elderly. One man earned his black belt at age seventy-two, and he certainly has not had the stretch and agility to make flying leaps for many years. Yet he had to meet the same standards of ability as any other black belt.

In "real life," someone trained in the martial arts is going to use rather simple, basic moves if attacked on the streets. This may mean blocking, then running. It may means a block and kick combination, or some other basic technique. All other activities just help keep the person limber, graceful, and in excellent cardiovascular condition regardless of his or her age. Even better, there is no difference in the method of training between male and female, making this a sport which everyone can enjoy.

Yet despite these facts, many people either hesitate to learn the martial arts or feel that they will never accomplish very much. "It is a young person's activity." "I could never fly through the air like Super Karate." "My reflexes have slowed with age." And on and on and on . . .

The reality of the martial arts, much as it is for boxing, is that there is as much mental as physical involvement required for your success. You must work out regularly. You must develop the ability to stretch your body as well as increasing your stamina. Yet such exercise is simple and can be taken at your own pace. When you are sparring with another person of equal ability, as you will do in most classes, age can work to your advantage. A young person will have fast reflexes, but an older person is more likely to outthink his or her opponent. A beginner of forty is going to master the art of recognizing what an opponent might do, changing position as the technique is being applied so that he or she can duck, block, counter, or otherwise do what is appropriate. A younger person will rely on speed, often working harder than necessary because he or she has not learned to outthink an opponent. Thus an older person can often provide endless surprises to an opponent who is relying upon speed to win.

Both the younger and the older martial arts enthusiast can obviously benefit from improving their mental attitude. A positive subconscious conditioning can take you well beyond what you think are your present abilities, regardless of your age and physical limitations.

The Conditioning Process

Both boxing and the martial arts require similar conditioning programs, even though the martial arts are more easily mastered and enjoyed for life by men and women. Boxing is inherently dangerous when practiced professionally. The idea behind competition is to cause enough trauma to your opponent so that he is rendered unconscious (the knockout). Amateur boxers and people who enjoy boxing for fun will usually wear head protectors to prevent a knockout or other damage. Yet even under such conditions there is enough physical violence so that few people enjoy boxing much after the age of thirty-five. This is especially true of professional fighters who routinely are at their peak during their early twenties.

Martial arts are not so violent as boxing, even though the blows and kicks can be far more devastating than those used by boxers. Karate kicks, for example, are meant to shatter ribs and other bones. Hand techniques can easily penetrate an opponent, causing serious injury or death. Yet the idea of competition in the martial arts is to demonstrate control. The higher the rank, the more sophisticated the techniques, the greater the control the competitor must exhibit. He or she trains so that a kick to the head is automatically stopped at a point just short of contact. Hand techniques are likewise timed so that they do not make contact with the body or are so controlled that the contact is a harmless fraction of the power unleashed at the start of the blow. Even body throws are planned so that the attacker controls the opponent's fall so that there is no injury.

It is the goal of developing controlled techniques which makes the martial arts popular with all ages. This is why many health clubs have added Tae Kwon Do, kung fu, or some other martial arts to their programs. This is also why the elderly are often enjoying what might otherwise have seemed an activity for the extremely agile young.

The physical conditioning is important. You will never go farther than your body can handle. One business executive likes to go to the gym three times a week to box. He works out, spars, and has a good time. His body is in excellent condition, and I am certain he could hold his own if attacked on the street. Yet this man could not stand up against a champion who trains several hours a day, seven days a week.

Self-hypnosis is not going to turn you into the best athlete in the world. It will change your subconscious attitudes and help you improve your existing skills beyond what you thought possible. It will also help you train professionally as a boxer if that is your goal.

The martial arts section, which follows that on boxing, will be of greater interest because the various forms are enjoyed by so many people. Again, you will not become an instant champion if you do not have the physical conditioning. Yet this is an activity where the mental attitude of the subconscious mind is a critical factor for success. You will learn how to achieve this, and thus greatly improve your perform-ance in competition.

Boxing

There are several factors necessary for improving your ability as a boxer. Most important is having the right mental attitude so that you are not shaken by the image of your opponent.

The first stage is to learn to relax in the ring. You will want to use such suggestions under self-hypnosis as:

"I am a well-trained athlete. I have developed my body to the best of my ability. I have learned to block, duck, and punch. I am as good as my opponent and will use the competition to show an exchange of skills. I will relax and enjoy this challenge."

Notice that all the positive suggestions do not stress winning. Boxing is by its nature a highly competitive sport. Yet if you focus solely on winning, any setback within the ring will often shatter your belief in yourself. If you suggest that you will win a fight that is important to you, then get knocked down in the first fifteen seconds of the first round, you may have trouble retaining the subconscious programming. That blow may do more to create negative thoughts than all the positive suggestions you may have developed for weeks.

Instead of having winning as the goal, you should work toward blocking and seeking openings. You should also allow for possible mistakes. Thus you might suggest:

"I am going to block my opponent's blows. Each time he breaks through my defensees, I am going to learn something about his technique. I am going to be a better fighter with each passing round because I will know his strategy and his weaknesses. I will be able to exploit his weaknesses, knowing that when he does break through my defenses, I will have gained knowledge that will help me fight him more effectively."

Other suggestions might include: "I will be calm as I box, relaxed, happy to be in the ring. I will be watching for openings and take advantage of them when I see them. But I will always enjoy exchanging my skills. I will work to land a blow whenever I have the opportunity, and I will be ever more alert to those opportunities with each round. I will be in control of myself, calmly handling everything my opponent tries and learning from each blow I fail to avoid."

You can see how such suggestions, and you should modify them for your own circumstances, will help keep you from letting negative thoughts dominate your action. If you get knocked down in the ring, you will not see that blow as giving your opponent an advantage. Instead you will have learned his strategy and the necessary changes in defense you must use. You will feel good about your increased ability to win now that you have seen the flaw in the way you were performing in the ring.

This positive approach is far superior to using self-hypnosis to convince yourself you will win. Too often such an approach leads to an all-or-nothing attitude which cannot survive a setback from a lucky punch or a strategic move you had not anticipated. The reprogramming of the subconscious can be lost when you are struck harder than expected, even though you might otherwise have been able to win.

You also will want to work on aspects of your technique. Is roadwork difficult for you? Then use some of the suggestions in Chapter 7, applying them to roadwork rather than just running as an end in itself. You can tell yourself that you will feel stronger, be breathing easier, and enjoy yourself more the longer you are running. You can tell yourself that with each passing day, you are gradually increasing your stamina. Such positive suggestions will increase your breathing power and make your training much simpler.

Do you have trouble lasting fifteen rounds? The longer you hold your hands in the air, the heavier they seem to become because of muscle fatigue. Yet a boxer must rise above this very natural problem. One way is to make such suggestions as:

"With each passing round, I seem to gain renewed strength and energy. The longer I fight my opponent, the more I feel a constant surge of new power which enables me to be effective. Should I get knocked down, I will arise with greater alertness and control. My hands will feel stronger, my arms comfortable in a defensive position."

Some boxers will go so far as to reinforce their subconscious between rounds, making suggestions as they wait for the bell. Because of the limited time and the need to listen to the trainer, this is often not possible, so the bulk of your subconscious reprogramming should be done before the fight.

It is possible to box while in a state of self-hypnosis, though I do not advise it. You can greatly increase your abilities in this manner since you are able to concentrate more fully on the techniques you need to win. However, there can be problems arising which you might not anticipate, problems which should be avoided.

The reaction to the crowd noise is typical. If you are boxing and suddenly are knocked down, you may hear people shouting: "You're a loser." "The fight is rigged." "You're a bum." And other comments, all derogatory, will be heard all around. Because you are in a state of hypersuggestibility, you may come to believe the negatives. You may feel that you have lost a fight or that losing is inevitable. Instead of being at your best, you actually may give up without realizing that is what you are doing.

It is far better to anticipate problems and work on your subconscious before you enter the ring. One professional boxer told me, "I know the crowd's going to hate me. I win too much. Everybody likes the underdog, and I'm at the peak right now.

"What I do just before the fight is use that hypnosis you taught me. I tell myself I am not going to hear the crowd. I am only going to be aware of my opponent. No matter what people shout, it will be like background music that has no effect on me. I will concentrate only on the guy I'm trying to beat.

"That way I don't get shaken. I've talked with some of the other guys, and they really get messed up when the crowd goes against them. But I just don't hear any of that. If I get beat, it's going to be because the guy outfought me, not because some punk in the front row got me rattled talking about my mother."

You can also use self-hypnosis to improve individual punches. You can suggest that your left hook is becoming stronger, more powerful, and more accurate, for example. You can tell yourself that you will begin anticipating blows sooner, giving yourself a better chance to avoid the blows or block the power coming at you.

Visualization is harder with boxing because there are fewer aspects to anticipate. When you are training, you can visualize yourself running more easily during roadwork. You can imagine yourself standing happily at the end of every round, reinforcing the idea that you always will be able to go the distance, regardless of who might win the match.

When training professionally for an opponent, you may be able to fantasize counters to the techniques he uses. Obtain video tapes or films of your opponent's fights. Observe the techniques he uses, and mentally work on counters, blocks, and avoidance techniques. If your opponent regularly gives slight openings, visualize yourself in the ring when he gives such an opening, then imagine yourself making the counter before he can cover up again.

Work on each aspect of your opponent's strengths and weaknesses, but do not mentally work through a complete strategy for victory while under hypnosis. The reality of professional fights is that your opponent is probably studying you just as you are studying him. He may feel the need to radically change his style to beat you. He may go from a technique of early avoidance in the first rounds, playing with the opponent and scoring points, to a technique where he starts hard and fast, trying for a knockout in the first two minutes. Or a hard puncher in the first rounds may change to a different technique, exchanging blows more easily and wearing you down slowly. If you concentrate on a complete strategy, you may be thrown by any change. But if you plan on strong points and openings, taking them one at a time, you will be better prepared no matter what is thrown at you and no matter when the blows occur.

Martial Arts

The martial arts actually encompass several areas of concern. First there are the forms, which help teach you grace, balance, control, and combinations of techniques. Then there is one-step sparring, which teaches you timing and combinations. Finally there is free sparring, in which you exchange techniques, using carefully controlled blows to gain enough points to win. The latter is the equivalent to boxing but without the same blows being allowed because of the greater danger.

A fairly new sport is that of full contact karate, which combines elements of kick boxing, regular boxing, and karate. Blows are limited to prevent serious injury, some padding is required to reduce their effectiveness, but knockouts are possible and permissible. Most of the subconscious reprogramming necessary for full contact karate is identical to that of boxing.

The greatest problem with forms is remembering the moves so that they come naturally and you can concentrate on other elements such as balance, speed, grace, and power. To aid your memory, use the relaxation techniques you learned in Chapter 3. Then tell yourself that you will learn the form quickly and easily. Each time you practice it, you will find that the movements feel more natural. You will find yourself going through the form with greater skill.

Next mentally picture someone doing the form in the way you want to achieve. Usually this will be your instructor or some other black belt whose skills you have admired. As discussed with other sports, you will imagine yourself superimposed over the instructor's body. You will picture yourself making the identical movements with the identical skills.

Should you be unable to visualize in this manner, a problem many people have, just think through the techniques as they were taught. Tell yourself how you will make each move, turn, punch, block, kick, etc. This will work just as effectively.

Eventually you will become more skilled with the forms for your level of training. You will find that there are days when you are able to achieve the form as perfectly as the person you were using for your role model. When this occurs, you will want to incorporate that experience into your hypnosis session.

After placing yourself into a state of self-hypnosis, visualize yourself completing the form in the manner you achieved when you did it so well. Remember how your body felt, your sense of balance, the sensations in your muscles. Then duplicate these sensations in your mind as you mentally work through the form. You will find that the reinforcing of these sensations and technique will translate into practice.

Should you have trouble visualizing all this but you can remember how your body felt, try talking through the form and telling yourself the body sensations. This will greatly aid you with your form when you again put the techniques into practice.

Sparring in the martial arts is often an area where your nervousness can affect your performance. Place yourself into a state of self-hypnosis, and begin suggesting such positive concepts as:

"I will be increasingly relaxed as I walk on the floor. I will find myself growing calm, alert, and able to move quicker and more effectively as the sparring begins. My breathing will be controlled, and I will increasingly be able to anticipate my opponent's moves." "I will have an easier time blocking and countering on the floor as the time progresses. I will find myself in greater control, calmer, more at peace as the sparring continues."

As you become more relaxed with your suggestions, you can begin working on specific areas of concern or general techniques which will help you with your sparring. These can be quite specific, such as:

"I will move in close to a taller opponent to make it more difficult for him or her to have the advantage of his or her longer legs." "I will move back from a shorter opponent to take advantage of my longer legs." "I will move at forty-five-degree angles to my opponent to throw my opponent off guard and give me an easier escape." "I will block and counter when my opponent gives me an opening after using an attack technique against me." Obviously these are all rather basic concepts, but repeating them under self-hypnosis will reinforce your training on the floor.

You can also work on strategy for the martial arts, just as was suggested for boxing. Again you want to make certain that your suggestions are specific, rather than planning a general strategy against an opponent whose sparring technique may vary from past sparring techniques you have encountered. You can visualize various attacks and counters, preparing yourself to respond automatically to whatever moves your opponent makes.

If the martial art you practice include take downs and falls, you will want to use visualization techniques recalling each successful move you have made. Try to remember the way your feet were placed and your body balanced, and the sensations within your muscles as you felt your opponent lose his or her balance. Then recreate these throws in your mind, sensing the physical reactions you experienced. Again, if visualization is difficult for you, talk yourself through these experiences.

Perhaps the best-known aspect of martial arts is actually the least important. This is the breaking of boards with various foot and hand techniques. Such board breaking is extremely impressive but is usually meant only to show power, focus, and technique after a martial artist has mastered the basics. In some organizations, board breaking is not begun until just before the black-belt level because it is felt that the basics are far more important to learn.

To aid yourself with board breaking, there are only two areas you need for concentration. The first is the mental preparedness of technique. You will want to suggest to yourself the proper hand or foot position for each break. For example, you will want to be certain your fist is twisting for extra power as you approach the impact and that your fist is positioned so you do no damage to your joints. A kick requires the foot to be angled properly, and other breaks also require the proper positioning. Again, thinking of a perfect break you have witnessed will help your technique. Remember to mentally substitute yourself for the role model when under self-hypnosis.

The other technique you will want to utilize is the mental focus. You are always striking a point just past the board(s) you want to break. You should practice this mental technique under self-hypnosis, giving yourself such suggestions as: "I will always strike through my target [the boards]. I will be relaxed, my eyes focused past the boards, my fist [foot, knife, hand, etc.] striking properly through the board. I will have maximum power as I go through the board, my body positioned for comfort and accuracy. Should the board not break, I will use the experience to improve my technique, getting better and more accurate each time."

There may be other areas on which you wish to work, but the techniques will be the same. Positive suggestions under self-hypnosis coupled with physical practice and visualization methods when possible will result in your exceeding what you once thought were the limits of your ability. You will get better, be more proficient with both forms of sparring, and easily exceed your personal expectations from the past.

Weight lifting and body building

9

Weight lifting and body building have become among the most popular individual activities for many Americans. Once this type of training was achieved in aging gyms which had an endless array of weights, rather disreputable-looking lockers, mirrors which were usually cracked in several places, and an aroma familiar to every mother whose children bring home dirty gym clothes only once a year. Today there are many ways to obtain such training. There are exercise centers, such as those employing the Nautilus method, which may have highly sophisticated machines for individual muscle development. There are health clubs and far more modern gyms, some of which have the traditional weights and others of which have both weights and specialized machines for training.

Body building is also no longer an exclusively male activity. Numerous women have entered the field, discovering that the way the female body develops during training is extremely sexy and far more curved than the male. Their increased strength actually improves the beauty they have enjoyed rather than making them seem "muscle-bound."

Weight lifting has also interested both men and women. One of the major goals of weight lifters is to be able to lift weights heavier than their bodies. Competition is based on the size of the weight lifter, men and women competing separately.

The popularity of the sport has also led to much mythology. The only way to succeed is to (choose one): Take steroids. Eat a high-protein diet rich in raw eggs, rare meat, and muscle fiber. Take hormones. Bribe and/or sleep with the judge, depending upon the sex of all involved.

The reality is quite different. The human body is seven to nine times stronger than we think. We use only a fraction of our inherent power, no matter what physical condition we are in.

Wait a minute. Don't jump at me for making one of those dumb statements that therapists are so prone to spout. I, too, am amused when someone spouts the "fact" that we only use 10 percent (or 20 percent or whatever) of our brain's capacity and that even an Einstein has only used 4 or 5 percent more. Obviously such an estimate has to be based on the knowledge of what 100 percent of our brain power happens to be, and no one knows that. If you don't know 100 percent, how can you know what a fraction of it might be? However, when it comes to body building and strength, we do have proof.

For example, fairly regularly you will read a news story about someone like ninety-three-pound Mrs. Sylvia Hoggenfarth. She is a frail housewife living in some community where the only exercise she gets is climbing in and out of the car. Mrs. Hoggenfarth is calmly standing in her kitchen, baking an apple pie, when she suddenly hears a scream. She looks out a window and sees that her son, Big Frankie Hoggenfarth, a six foot two inch, 225-pound high school student, has just been crushed by the car whose engine he was attempting to tune. The car, a 1970s Chevy with high-powered engine, had been braced on some blocks, then slipped off while the youth was underneath.

Without thinking, Mrs. Hoggenfarth races out the door and grabs the bumper of the car. She lifts it, holding it while Big Frankie painfully crawls out from under it. Then she eases it down, calls the ambulance, and cradles her son's head waiting for help. Only later does anyone notice that Mrs. Hoggenfarth is completely unhurt. Her back was not injured, she has no torn muscles or ligaments, and everything is fine. Yet the car weighed in excess of 2000 pounds, more than twenty times her weight.

Three factors come into play when someone acts in an extraordinary manner such as the hypothetical Mrs. Hoggenfarth. First, there is a rush of adrenalin in the body, causing the person to act. This adrenalin rush helps her to utilize the full power of her body when she (or he) must lift the extremely large weight.

Second, there is the mental factor. The person who is as obsessed with lifting the car as the woman whose child is trapped underneath thinks of nothing but the rescue. There is no thought of the obstacles which might prevent such a successful rescue. Mrs. Hoggenfarth did not say to herself, "I am but a frail, ninety-three-pound woman who suffers from arthritis and the occasional heartbreak of psoriasis. That car weighs more than twenty times what I do. I haven't exercised in years except for scrubbing the floors, which I try to avoid doing more often than once every decade. There is no way that I can run out and save my son. I will have to call for help and hope a wrecking crane arrives in time." Instead, she saw only the problem and knew that the solution was for her to go out and lift the car. The potential problems with such an action were never considered.

Third, she lifted correctly, her back straight, her legs positioned properly, her knees bent properly to avoid tearing muscles and ligaments. This correct lifting is instinctive, though normally we are not aware of it and often have to be shown the proper methods when taking weight training.

There are occasional stories of this type where the person doing the lifting does not lift correctly. The individual is so intent on the rescue that the damage is not felt until later. But there are records of broken backs, torn muscles, and other fairly serious injuries. However, even under these circumstances, the reality is that the person lifted the weight, which would otherwise be "impossible" to accomplish.

What does this mean? Simply that we do have proof that our bodies are capable of far greater feats of strength than we realise. The mythical Mrs. Hoggenfarth, who does have her counterparts in reality, quite possibly has to let her son or husband take the turkey from the oven on Thanksgiving because the weight is too great for her. But this need is not physical. It is psychological. She knows that the turkey is heavy, and she is convinced that she is not strong. Yet when she had to act instead of analyzing her ability to act, she was able to easily lift the massive car.

The Negatives of Weight Lifting

Every time you stand before a room filled with weights, you have a tendency to tell yourself all the negatives. "I'll never be as strong as . . ." "I can't lift anything that heavy." "I know my best bench press ever and I certainly will never go beyond that." "He [or she] is so good, I'll never match his [or her] lifts."

Or you go to equipment such as Nautilus and say, "I'll never be able to go more than five repetitions with that weight. It's too heavy for me." "You want me to try the extra ten pounds? You've got to be kidding. I have enough trouble doing the minimum with the weight I'm using now." And on and on go the excuses. We constantly create a negative program for the subconscious.

Perhaps the saddest part of this negative programming is that we have retained it for so long. Depending upon your age, you might remember the old myths which were accepted as fact. "If a woman begins lifting weights, her muscles will be just as bulky as a man's." "Body building for women can destroy your ability to have a baby." "The only people who are any good at lifting weights are those who are stupid. The more intelligent you are, the less you can develop your muscles."

Such myths about weight lifters and body builders sound humorous today. We all know better than to accept such meaningless stereotypes. Yet we have not reached the level of maturity where we recognize the true potential (proven over and over again) of the body when the mind has the right attitude.

Many internationally famous weight lifters have been embarrassed by revelations that they use steroids. They are trying to alter their body chemistry so they can be stronger. In fact, many see steroids as a necessary crutch. They are convinced that unless they take them they will never be able to lift so much weight as they would with them. Thus top contenders with the potential to be Olympic champions may drop out of most competition because they are not allowed to use steroids.

Fortunately, the reality is that you can change your subconscious programming, you can use your muscles more effectively. You will be able to lift weights closer to the limits of your ability, which means a radical increase in apparent strength over what you are doing now.

Caution: The techniques you are going to learn will increase your weight-lifting ability, perhaps severalfold. However, you must not instantly put this to the test after you have reprogrammed your subconscious mind. Instead, you should gradually increase the weight load to a level where you are working with heavier weights than you would expect for your apparent development level. This will be faster than with normal training methods, but must still be gradual, as you are working on changing your subconscious mind.

The reason for this is that each increase in weight load brings physical dangers. For example, suppose you are handling your present weight load slightly incorrectly. Your body balance is not quite what it should be. You do not have the best distribution of weight to avoid injury. Yet all of this has gone unnoticed because you are strong enough to compensate with the weight you are using.

A sudden shift to a much greater weight, perhaps the addition of fifty pounds or more, could be extremely dangerous. If you are off balance, you can injure your back, cause muscle damage, or hurt some other part of your body. This same risk exists with any weight increase over what you are using at the moment, but you will sense the problem because you do damage when using a lighter weight addition. You will be able to shift your balance and develop proper techniques before making greater increases in weights. The slower change may be frustrating, especially since you will have the ability to lift more than ever, but it will enable you to lift without risk of injury.

Reprogramming Your Subconscious

The first stage in reprogramming your subconscious is to learn to relax when lifting and in competition. The reason for this is to greatly reduce the chance for injury and to allow maximum use of your strength. If you are tense when in competition, it will affect your performance. This is also true in competitive body building, but the only concern is that you will look rather stiff. You are not going to injure yourself with such an action.

Start by letting yourself relax and entering into a state of self-hypnosis as described in Chapter 3. Now think only about weight lifting. Think of how you feel and move when you are relaxed and enjoying what you are doing.

Next begin making suggestions to yourself to help you with both practice and competition. "I enjoy lifting weights. I get pleasure from the way my body feels when I am in balance, relaxed, my breathing correct as I start to lift the weight." Each suggestion is meant to help you relax and be in a proper position for the type of lift or press you are going to do.

If you are able to visualize your technique, picture yourself lifting ever heavier weights, always relaxed and enjoying yourself. If you have lifted an unusually heavy weight for your present conditioning and have done it comfortably and successfully, try to remember how your body felt at that time. Try to remember the way your muscles reacted and the balance shifts of your body as you grasped the weight, taking it over your head or pressing it from the bench. Tell yourself how you will repeat this action with ever increasing weights, always feeling the body shifts you remember.

If you do not recall a time when everything went perfectly for your lifts, think about someone you have watched, either where you work out or on a televised competition. Do you know of someone whose lifts are masterpieces in movement and control? Visualize this person as you remember him or her making the lift, then picture your head and body in place of the individual you are recalling. Now you are fantasizing yourself making a proper lift of a heavier weight, always relaxed, always calm.

Before competition you can enhance this earlier work by entering the state of self-hypnosis and stating such suggestions as: "I enjoy competition. The closer I come to having to make my lift, the more I relax. My mind focuses on the technique I am going to use. As I step to the weight, I am relaxed, in balance, my adrenalin flowing in a controlled manner to my muscles so that when I start to lift, I am using maximum body strength with my technique. My lift will be smooth, powerful, controlled. Each lift will be better than the previous. Each lift will be handled to the best of my ability right now."

Do not set a specific goal for yourself. You do not want to tell yourself that you are going to dead lift 300 pounds when your best previous lift was 212 pounds. Yes, your body is capable of such a feat, but the change in your competition strength will be gradual. You have to reprogram yourself slowly, looking toward steady improvement rather than attempting to be an instant Superbody.

There is also the fact that on any given day of competition you may be tired, have some muscle soreness, or otherwise not be in the same shape as you were during a recent practice. Your goal is to achieve the most you can accomplish that day, even if this is less than you might otherwise lift.

You are also looking for gradual improvement. I cannot caution you enough that no matter what your body is capable of lifting, you must always learn to handle the new weights. A slight balance problem may not affect you when you're pumping 150 pounds, but it can be quite serious if you use that identical technique with 200 pounds. Thus you need to use your new control of your inner strength only in combination with proper training techniques. You will move quickly through ever greater weights, but you must use sensible training methods in order to learn the balance and coordination needed to lift without risk of injury.

Competitive Body Building

The technique for preparing for competitive body building is different from that for competitive weight lifting. Your training sessions are similar, and you can use the subconscious programming for improving your lifting and conditioning techniques. However, the competition does not require lifting but rather the display of the body for form, grace, and movement.

Relax yourself and enter the state of self-hypnosis as already described. Once again issue positive suggestions to guide yourself through a state of relaxation during competition. "I enjoy competition. I enjoy standing on the stage and doing my routine. I am increasingly relaxed as my turn comes. My mind is alert. I review my routine and am relaxed as I start to do it. I will move smoothly from pose to pose, enjoying showing my body, enjoying the reaction of the crowd, taking pride in what I have accomplished. I will not worry about anyone else. I will enjoy their skills and take pleasure in showing my own."

Next, visualize your routine if you can, or talk yourself through the routine you are planning if visualizing is difficult for you. Picture yourself during your best posing session. Remember how your body felt as you went through your routine. Try to sense the fluid motion as you go from pose to pose in your mind. And always tell yourself that this is the way you are going to move during the competition. You will be relaxed, accomplishing the best of what you have been practicing.

The results of all this effort will be obvious in competition. Your routine will lose any awkwardness which can come from being too conscious of the moves you have to make. Instead of having to think about each pose and the transitions which allow you to gain points, you will move easily, naturally, as though you take such positions all the time.

You will also lose the psychologically destructive force of thinking about how good everyone else might be. Instead of constantly trying to compete, you will simply enjoy their skills and not weigh your own against theirs. This new confidence in what you do will prevent you from doing less than your best because you have been unnerved by their actions.

If body building is your main sports interests, you should also read the chapter on running. Just as it is important to learn the proper relaxation and balance techniques for weight lifting, so you must also be certain to protect your body from its destructive nature. Lifting weights may enhance your outward appearance and your physical strength, but it also is a constant stress on your cardiovascular system. A proper weight-training program is always coupled with a physical activity which improves your heart and lungs. This might be running each day or even taking an extremely rapid walk for several miles at a time. Such cardiovascular conditioning will result in a perfect body inside as well as out.

How your opponent will work against you

10

No matter which individual sport you enjoy, when you are in competition there is a psychological game being played against you by your opponent. This is most often seen in the field of boxing, as was discussed earlier in this book. The "fight of the century" seems to take place at least once a week. Every month, someone is the "greatest," "strongest," "just like Ali," "better than Ali," or whatever. And once a year, someone is the "great [white, black, brown] hope!" But this type of psychological pressure is blatant and well covered earlier in the book. There are more subtle games played which can upset your mental conditioning if you are not expecting them.

Tennis is a good example of a game where psychology is used as a subtle weapon. Have you ever noticed some of the tricks of the professionals? A few years ago, the gimmick was to have a specially designed racket which was shaped a little oddly compared with conventional equipment. The materials used for the construction might be metal instead of wood, and if the metal became popular, then it had to be a space-age metal. The different size and shape gave the player an "edge" over all competition, regardless of whether or not the person actually could play any better than before. Reality was not important. Just the image of the type of racket being carried was important, despite the fact that no one really did seem to play much better and the controversy lasted only one season.

Another tennis ploy is to bounce the ball before serving. Some players are masters of this strategy. They will bounce the ball for ten or fifteen minutes, seemingly warming up, then suddenly serve. The reality is that often the opponent who is waiting for the serve will become anxious about what is happening. He or she will begin concentrating on the bouncing ball, wondering when the warm-up exercise will stop. Then, when it doesn't cease, a degree of anger and tension may develop. The opponent is waiting to react to a serve that seems destined never to come. By the time the serve is made, the opponent is tense, adrenalin is flowing, and the response may not be effective.

Baseball is another sport in which psychological games are played. Remember when you were a child and first starting to play? There was always great credibility given to the skills of the boy or girl who owned a glove before anyone else did. The mitt they brought to the sandlot and backyard games established them as the "experts." You knew you could never play as well as they could because they had that magical piece of equipment. It was tremendously discouraging, and you never realized that the only difference between you and the person with the glove was that the child with the glove had a parent willing to shell out the money.

Baseball superstitions become much more involved when the players get older. A pitcher can rub his face before throwing the ball, and right away the batter may tense, knowing that something special has been placed on the ball to give it a curve, drop, or whatever. Again the player tenses, the pitcher's action creating an atmosphere in which the batter knows a trick ball is coming. The nervousness diminishes the batter's ability to react, and he may miss entirely or hit it in a less controlled manner. Yet all the pitcher is doing is making a gesture to imply something unusual. The hitter is giving the pitcher power which would not otherwise exist.

Golfers often play on each other's weaknesses. Have you ever listened to a particularly skilled psychological strategist observing a player who is about to putt? Suppose the ball is three inches from the cup. A light tap should suffice to put it in and let the golfer lead on strokes. The opponent may quietly say, "I'll put you down for two strokes. You know how you always choke short putts, knocking them past the cup on your first try." This is said before the golfer takes the club for what should have been an easy point. He or she is so busy thinking about past failures, real or imagined, that concentration is off and the ball does go past the rim.

A different approach may be used with a longer putt. "Look at the break on that tie. Even compensating, no one can take less than two or three shots for this one. It's the toughest putt on this whole course." The fact that the opponent may have had a ball in the same place, sinking it with one putt, means nothing to the golfer. The warning takes control, and concentration is thrown off.

Bowlers have their own way of mental harassment. Watch some-one start a game with a strike. "Oh, that's too bad. I mean, it was a great strike. You found the pocket perfectly. But you know how it's always downhill when you start with a strike. I've seen plenty of bowlers break 200 starting off with maybe five or six pins down on that first frame. But when they start with a strike. . . . Well, it was a great shot, but I hope I'm not so lucky."

Or there is an average game, then two or three strikes in a row with at least another two or three frames left to play. "God, you must feel really tense. You make a strike, and you feel really good about yourself. You make another, and you know it's kind of a fluke. But when you get that third, everybody's watching you. They're kind of waiting for you to make a mistake. The pressure's really on you. I mean, you could have the best game of your life, and everybody's staring at the way you're rolling that ball. I'm glad I won't be in your shoes when you go up to roll that ball. I'm glad I can just sit back here and watch you like everybody else."

You get the idea. There is the deliberate creation of tension for the players through playing up on superstition and fears. It happens with every sport. The appoaches may vary with the game and the players. The language may be different. It is the end result which matters.

The solutions to such problems come from programming the subconscious to handle this stress. I am devoting a separate chapter to this problem because it is one you will face with every sport, and there is no sense in repeating it over and over again.

The first step in handling the psychological games of others is to experience them. Usually it is difficult to anticipate what someone else may try until you have either observed the game regularly or been an active participant. Thus you may have to experience a few frustrations before you know what you need to counter.

The emotion most commonly triggered as the result of psychological games is anger. As a result of this anger, you may experience any combination of fear, depression, or other emotions, but the root emotion to deal with is anger. After describing the anger, I will show you how to protect yourself from it.

Anger is one of the most dangerous emotions you can experience as an athlete. Your adrenalin begins to flow, you experience the fight-or-flight syndrome, yet you know you cannot move very much from where you are. You are a helpless victim, watching someone bounce a ball, go through contortions on the pitcher's mound, or otherwise do something which upsets you. Your body tenses, you forget the game and begin focusing on the opponent's actions.

The easiest way to counter anger is to prepare yourself for the specific situation you are facing. For example, suppose your problem is the tennis player who endlessly bounces a ball before starting to serve. Prior to the game, place yourself into a state of self-hypnosis. Completely relax, then make such suggestions as:

"I will be relaxed with my opponent on the tennis courts. Whenever the other player begins to delay the game by bouncing the ball, I will focus on the serve to come. I will be relaxed, anticipating from where my opponent is standing the direction the ball might take. I will feel comfortable waiting, becoming more and more alert for the serve.

"When my opponent does serve the ball, I will be confident of my ability to handle it. I will move naturally into position and be able to swing smoothly at the ball with my racket if the ball is within bounds. Instead of becoming more tense with each bounced ball, I will find myself more alert, more relaxed, even better able to return the serve. And if the other player doesn't bounce the ball. I will also be alert, relaxed, able to respond swiftly and effectively."

You can also defuse the psychological games by reinforcing your own skills. "Each time my opponent tries to upset me by bouncing the ball (bringing in a new racket, or whatever else is used), I will recognize that he or she is not confident of his or her game. My opponent is concerned that I will win because I am a challenge. I will feel more confident, more relaxed, in greater control each time my opponent tries to upset me. I will be alert to the game and find myself able to better play whenever my opponent tries to upset me.

"If my opponent decides not to try upsetting me, I will know that my opponent also respects my skills. I will know that my opponent does not want to waste time trying to upset me, and this knowledge will make me stronger, more relaxed, a better player."

You want to cover all possibilities when facing an opponent who normally tries psychological games against you. Sometimes a player will use these tricks routinely. At other times the player will be selective, using them with the opponents he or she thinks might be a challenge and not using them when they seem to do no good.

If you have had extensive negative conditioning, and many sports enthusiasts are basically negative in their attitudes as we discussed in the first chapter, then you will want to prepare yourself for such subconscious reactions. Typically, someone may routinely use psychological games with various players. When this opponent faces you, he or she may decide not to use any tricks because the player feels that you will not respond to them. This is a sign of respect, but this is not the way your negatively programmed subconscious mind may react. Instead, you may be telling yourself, "I know why he isn't bouncing the balls [or using whatever other psychological game you have come to expect]. He knows I am an inferior player. He knows he can beat me without the games. I'm just a nobody on the court, and he's going to destroy me. I don't know why I ever agreed to play against him in the first place."

The reality could be anything. You could be playing against an expert who is having an off day. You could be playing against someone who stopped using the psychological games because they never worked. You could even be up against someone who is so superstitious about the play that when he or she forgets to use the games prior to the first service, the player feels all is lost. "I forgot to bounce the ball before the first serve. It doesn't matter that I took the point. I only win when I bounce the ball a lot before the first service. I might as well give up. Trying to win now is going to be a hopeless task."

Even worse than this situation is what occurs when you and your opponent are negative. You have decided that you are no good because your opponent, who routinely uses tricks to enhance his position, used no tricks against you. At the same time, your opponent has decided that he will lose because he forgot the tricks. Both of you are giving up the game. You both will play poorly, at least until one of you scores an unexpected point. Then the attitude will shift, and that person will begin thinking, "I'm not so bad after all. I'm finally getting somewhere. My opponent misjudged me. I'm going to win this game."

It is because of all these negative images that it is important to add positive reinforcement for the player who chooses not to use a psychological game. You want to protect yourself no matter what happens.

The previous examples were based on a tennis game, but you can see that this same approach works for every other sport. Place yourself into a state of self-hypnosis, and make the same positive suggestions, modifying them only for the game you are playing and the way the opponent acts.

Handling Verbal Attacks

The verbal assault, such as occurs during golf and bowling, can best be handled with a similar approach. Some athletes who have become highly skilled in self-hypnosis like to reduce their ability to hear the comments. They train themselves so that the words of others become nothing more than background sounds they do not hear. The negative remarks thrown at them are like drifting clouds which pass without notice. However, this is fairly difficult and takes so much time that I do not recommend it. Instead, I feel that the same positive approach toward comments should be used as is used for other games.

Place yourself into a state of self-hypnosis. Then start making suggestions to yourself which will counter the negative assaults. "When my opponent starts to tell me what I can't do, I will recognize that he or she is afraid of my skills. He or she knows that I can make this putt. [Modify this so it is appropriate for whatever you are playing.] When he or she says something discouraging, I will relax even more. My concentration will become even greater, and I will be able to calmly, carefully make my stroke.

"If my opponent says nothing before my putt, I will know that he or she thinks I can do it with no difficulty. I will again relax, increase my concentration, and be able to handle the putt to the best of my ability."

Notice that you do not say that you will automatically make it. You may still make a mistake due to skill level, an unfamiliar playing area, a change in weather conditions, or some other factor. However, what you do not want to do is "choke" due to the tension someone else has created.

With the subtle pressure which can be exerted in a game such as bowling, you may wish to modify this situation slightly. You might make suggestions such as:

"Each time I roll a high score for my frame, I will remember how my body felt, where I faced my mark, and the way I moved as the ball went down the alley. Then each time I start to bowl again, my body will naturally assume this position. Each time I roll the ball will become easier, more natural than the last. No matter how many strikes or spares I make in a row, each new ball will see me relaxed, able to concentrate, my body reacting ever more naturally.

"If I do not knock down all the pins during my turn, my body will begin compensating for the mistake. My skill will improve each time.

"When I am doing well, I will recognize that any discouraging remarks are a sign of respect for my skills. The remarks will relax me even more. I will be able to concentrate better each time it is my turn. I will feel good about myself and be able to do my best each time."

Remember that these examples are all based on some of the most common circumstances regularly encountered. You can modify them all for the sport you play and the situations you are facing. The basic concepts are the same for every athletic activity.

Visualization

You can reinforce the suggestions you give yourself through visualization. You will want to see yourself facing the pressures that are created by your opponents, then overcoming them through the techniques described.

For example, if bowling is your sport, you will visualize yourself in the bowling alley. You will picture your score, which will have the first two or three frames normal for your average, then two strikes in a row. You will picture the other players being aware of your good fortune, making comments about the tension which they say is building for you.

Now picture yourself taking the ball and approaching your mark. Your body is relaxed. You can sense the same feelings, coordination, and eye-hand coordination you experienced when you made your strike. The more anyone says, the better you feel. You see yourself relaxing, rolling the ball properly, making a strike. And with that strike you are even more relaxed.

You see the scoring change, your new strike being added. You see your friends and the other bowlers taking their turns. You know they are joking with you about the pressure, but you feel wonderful. You continue to be relaxed, alert, confident of your ability to handle each ball to the best of your ability.

Again you mentally take your mark, your steps, swinging the ball, watching it move smoothly down the alley exactly as you desired. It is another strike. There is no tension. Rolling the ball correctly is the most natural experience you can imagine.

As you practice this exercise, you can vary your visual imagery. You may not picture a strike every time. You might picture some of the pins still standing after your first ball. Then you mentally roll the second ball, picking up the pins you missed so that you are left with a spare. This is still positive imagery, but now you are making certain that nothing in your conscious or subconscious mind will upset you. If you might be disturbed by not making a strike after you visualized it, then you should visualize other possibilities, always correcting any minor problem with your second ball.

The visualization method will be used for other sports and other problems. For example, you may picture yourself on the tennis court, facing an opponent who is constantly bouncing the ball before serving. You visualize yourself being relaxed, undisturbed by the delay.

Then you visualize your opponent preparing to serve, your body becoming even more relaxed, your mind alert, your reflexes set to respond to the best of your ability. If you can, try to remember how you felt the last time you effectively returned a strong or unusual serve. Mentally sense your body feeling the same way as you visualize shifting into position, bringing your racket back appropriately, and returning the serve.

You can carry this further, watching yourself immediately move into position for the return. Then you picture yourself handling the return comfortably and smoothly. You may wish to visualize the constant volleying, perhaps having yourself be able to place the balls so that your opponent is always run ragged, perhaps mentally having your opponent miss a return, giving you the game. Ideally, you will vary the approach, the important point being the handling of the comments.

Golf is the same matter. You visualize yourself in the middle of the game. There is the putt to be made and the comments about the difficulty. This time you feel yourself relaxing, observing the nature of the putt, the ground conditions, sensing any weather variables which might affect you, then calmly succeeding. You will visualize different partners, different putts, and as many different golf courses as you normally play. You always will see yourself as being able to handle any putt comfortably with the other players saying nothing. You will also see yourself staying in full control as they talk or make comments meant to alter your concentration. Then you will consistently make the putt.

You do the same techniques with each sport. You want to visualize the experience of success in the midst of problems. The specific needs will vary with the sport, but the general concepts presented here will work with all of them. Just modify them for your needs.

Reverse Psychology

"Now that I know how to counter the games my opponents have played with my mind, why can't I use them against them?" asked June, a supervisor in a government office and an avid tennis player. "I realize the techniques which have been used to upset me. I've learned to keep them from bothering me through self-hypnosis. But I know that the men and women I play against haven't taken my self-hypnosis work seriously. They haven't learned the kind of control and confidence I've gained. So what's wrong with me turning the tables on them? Should I use some of the tricks you've taught me to guard against?"

This question is one which has arisen with a number of my patients, and it is worth considering. You have always learned that actions you take and the words you choose when talking with an opponent can affect performance. Just as you might have been unnerved by a fellow bowler disparaging of your success after two or three strikes, so you can say the same words to your opponents. If you have been made uneasy by a tennis player bouncing the ball repeatedly before starting to serve, so can you bounce the ball. And so it goes, whether you are engaging in boxing, martial arts, weight lifting, golf, baseball, basketball, or any other sport.

The problem is that you have personally been against such actions. You have felt they were personally destructive, and you have used self-hypnosis to defuse their potential for harm. My feeling is that to duplicate such tactics would be improper. Even worse, you could use them as a crutch. Just as you unnerve the person attempting to play psychological games when you do not respond to them, so you can be unnerved if the game does not work when you try it. You might feel that the person is a far better player, knows more tricks than you do, and otherwise is going to destroy you simply because he or she did not respond as you once did.

My feeling is that you should concentrate on being positive in your actions, reprogramming your subconscious, then enjoying your sport without any tricks. You will be a better player, psychologically prepared for anything that happens, and will be able to take even greater pride in your accomplishments.

Team sports

11

Team sports present different challenges to you as a player than exist when you are on your own. You must be concerned not only with your personal performance on the court, playing field, etc., but also with interacting with your teammates. I remember one basketball coach at a high school which was known for having students who were high achievers, both scholastically and in their personal athletic endeavors. Each player on his team was extremely well motivated for success, but it was for individual success. The idea that the individual had to be a "winner" had become so ingrained in them that their ability to interact with others was limited. The coach commented, "I have five of the finest basketball players in the city. Now if I can just convince at least three of them to play together on any given night, we could start winning our games."

What does this mean to you? It means that you must reprogram your subconscious for three separate goals. One is to develop your skills for whatever position you play in the particular team sport you enjoy. The second is to develop your skills in relating to the primary person or persons with whom you must interact during a game. And the third is to develop a sense of the team in which your actions are meant to make the team look effective, not to enhance your image as a star.

Take football, for example. Suppose you want to be a quarterback. You will need to develop the ability to work well under extreme stress. You will need to know the plays, have an idea where the other plays will be, relax when eleven opposing players are trying to crush you into the ground, be able to pass quickly and accurately, and be able to run when all else fails and you have to stay on the ground. These skills are unique to you and require weight lifting, wind sprints, long-distance running, practice passing, and so forth.

Next you, as quarterback, just be able to accurately throw a ball to any distance. This means not only developing the strength for passing, which you will do on you own, but also working with a receiver who will run to different distances, at different angles, and even change directions frequently and unexpectedly, as will happen when the receiver is eluding blockers. You have to work at tossing the ball so that no matter how far the person runs, the ball always is within reach of the running receiver.

Finally, you as quarterback must learn to work with the team. You will have offensive linemen giving you cover, allowing the receiver to move, and so forth. There are times they will be overwhelmed, and you must run. There will be times when passing the ball to someone else will cause you to lose a bit of glory but may move the ball just enough further down the field so that you can win. Thus you must be willing not only to trust your team to carry out the protective measures needed to let you work, you also must be willing to reduce your glory if, by changing the pattern of what you do, you can help the team achieve a victory .

The same situation is true with every sport—basketball, baseball, soccer, hockey, and so forth. Even doubles tennis presents certain teamwork concerns, such as trying to arrange your strategy with your partner so that each of you lets your strongest ability dominate your defense. A tennis player with a weak backhand will ideally play so that his or her partner, who has a stronger backhand, covers the partner's backhand balls as well as his or her own.

There is also the problem for the coach. The coach must try to take each athlete, mold that individual to the limits of his or her ability, then take the skilled individuals and develop effective team interaction. This other concern is so great that there will be a section devoted to it later in this book. In addition, where appropriate, special suggestions will be given to coaches and trainers within the general text.

Mastering Plays and Strategy

Some team sports, such as football, have plays which must be learned and strategy which must be planned in advance. This adds a new dimension to the game beyond the physical endeavors when you play. You must be able not only to retain a fairly large number of play movements in your mind, you must be able to execute them on demand, your movements automatic as you concentrate on blocking, tackling, running for the ball, etc. Your ability to memorize can be altered by your nervousness and the responsiblity you are facing with the team.

In order to memorize the plays, take your play book home and find a place to relax. Place yourself into a state of self-hypnosis as described in Chapter 3. Next, begin giving yourself suggestions concerning the memorization of the plays.

"I am relaxed as I look at my play book. I am able to study the plays, learning them quickly and easily. Each time I study the plays, they become more and more ingrained in my memory. Each time I study the plays, I can concentrate more completely than ever before, committing them to memory." Or use other variations which will help you learn.

Next suggest how you will handle practice sessions and games. "When we have practice and a play is tried, my mind will remind me automatically where to go. I will not have to think about the play. I will be able to concentrate on my role with the team, my position, and the moves I am to make. I will be constantly aware of the actions of my opponents, able to maneuver to the best of my ability without having to consciously think about the plays I have memorized.

"When we play a game, I will be relaxed, enjoying the action, concentrating on my position and the movements I must make. I will play to the best of my ability, the signals called by the quarterback being part of my subconscious so that I do not have to worry about them. I will do my part, be constantly aware of my opponents, and respond automatically to whatever play is called."

You cannot use the visualization techniques so easily for mastering plays because the defense team's reaction will vary in each case. However, you can mentally work through several different game situations involving the plays or try to remember such plays as you have seen them executed when watching others compete. This may help you with your reaction times.

If You Are the Coach

You can help your team learn their plays faster by guiding them through what amounts to a self-hypnosis session conducted by you at the start of a practice session. You will probably not have the time to use a true hypnosis method unless you have had additional training or you have the team members learn the technique in Chapter 3. Instead, you will use aspects of the information in Chapter 3 to help the team relax.

Start by having the team lay down, ideally on mats such as you might have for gymnastics or wrestling. They should be on their backs, their eyes closed, preferably in a section of the gym where it is quiet.

The semicomfortable position suggested in Chapter 3 is ideal because, otherwise, some of the team members may fall asleep. However, this is not always possible. Some coaches have the team members take a sweat suit, roll it up, and place it under their heads so that their heads are propped at least twelve inches above their feet. They also have the team members remove their shoes and socks so that there is air circulating around their feet.

Now begin talking to team members in much the same way as you would use if you were doing a self-hypnosis exercise. They will have their hands resting on their thighs, their eyes closed, their minds drifting over their entire bodies.

"You begin to feel a sense of tingling physical relaxation moving through your hands. Just relax, and let yourself feel this tingling sensation relax your hands. The tingling is felt throughout your hands. They are becoming relaxed. Notice how comfortable they are. Your hands are completely relaxed.

"Now that tingling sensation is slowly moving from your hands into your thighs. You can feel this sensation in your thighs. Now it is going down through your knees, into the calves of your legs ... It is moving slowly, comfortably. Just let the tingling sensation flow through your body at its own pace. You are relaxed, always relaxed.

"The sensation is moving down into your ankles, into your feet, right up through your toes. Your feet are relaxing completely.

"Now concentrate on this relaxation at the tip of your toes. You can feel it throughout your toes, then moving down toward your heels. The relaxation is throughout your heels and spreading up to your ankles, through the calves of your legs, and up to your knees. You can feel the sensation of relaxation throughout your thighs, through your hips, all the way up to your waist. You can feel that the entire lower half of your body is now relaxed and comfortable. Relaxed and comfortable.

"Now concentrate on your stomach muscles. Feel them relaxing. Feel your stomach muscles letting go, become very loose, very limp, just letting go. You continue to concentrate on this relaxation, moving up to your chest area. And all the time you are relaxing, you are also becoming aware of your breathing.

"Now I want you to say the word 'confident' to yourself. Notice how you feel not only relaxed, but confident. You say the word, and you feel happy, certain of your abilities. You are confident about your ability to learn your position. You are confident about your ability to work successfully with the team. You feel confident.

"Inhale deeply through your mouth, saying the word 'confident,' experiencing the word 'confident,' then slowing exhaling through your nose. Inhale 'confident.' Then exhale. Inhale 'confident.' Then exhale.

"Now concentrate on relaxing the area under your arms. Feel that relaxation moving up into your back, encasing your entire back. You can feel your back pressing down into the mat as you relax. It is a wonderful feeling as you relax, and you can feel this relaxation moving up into your shoulders.

"Your shoulders become very limp and loose. You feel like a rag doll, and it is very relaxing.

"Concentrate on this feeling of relaxation. Notice how this feeling moves from your shoulders, into your neck, relaxing all your muscles, relaxing every fiber, every nerve and tissue in your neck? You are completely relaxing them now. You concentrate on this relaxation moving into your head area. You feel your entire head relaxing.

"You notice how this relaxation moves through your head. You relax all your facial muscles, your jaw muscles, and you allow the slight separation of your lips. You feel a slight dryness, and you may want to swallow. This is perfectly natural.

"You concentrate on this relaxation moving up into your eyelids, and your eyes have a tendency to roll up under your eyelids. You are very relaxed, and as you feel this sensation, say to yourself the words 'deep hypnotic sleep. Deep hypnotic sleep.' Say them to yourself. 'Deep hypnotic sleep.'

"Continue to concentrate on this relaxation moving into your scalp. You can feel your forehead relaxing, allowing your blood to circulate very freely. It is very close to the skin now.

"Breathe naturally, deeply, and with every breath you exhale, feeling very relaxed.

"Now you are going deeper into relaxation. Deeper. Deeper. And with every breath you inhale, you take great pleasure in this relaxation. And as you exhale, you let go, going deeper and deeper into hypnosis, enjoying every moment, now. You are enjoying every second as you go deeper and deeper.

"You are beginning to feel this inner peace, this inner calmness, and you like this feeling. You are going to allow this inner calmness to carry over into your daily life—in school, at home, on the playing field, with your friends. This inner calmness is going to become a part of your life.

"Now repeat those important words to yourself. 'Tingling,' and remember the tingling sensation which passed through your body, helping you to relax? 'Confident,' and remember how good it feels to be confident as you relax. 'Deep hypnotic sleep,' and remember how restful you feel, how at peace when you say these words. 'Tingling.' 'Confident.' 'Deep hypnotic sleep.' 'Tingling.' 'Confident.' 'Deep hypnotic sleep.' 'Each time you say these words to yourself, you will sleep soundly and deeply. Each time you will go deeper than the time before. 'Tingling.' 'Confident.' 'Deep hypnotic sleep.'

"Now imagine yourself standing at the top of a staircase, looking down twenty steps. As you count down from twenty to zero, each number will represent a step taking you deeper into relaxation, deeper into self-hypnosis.

"Now begin going down those steps. Twenty, 19, 18, 17, 16, 15, 14, deeper and deeper now. Thirteen, 12, 11, 10, 9, 8, deeper and deeper now. Seven, 6, 5, 4, 3, 2, 1. Deeper asleep now. Deeper. Deeper.

"Notice how you are learning to control this state of self-hypnosis.

You are beginning to feel that you have a definite advantage over most other athletes. You are gaining access to your subconscious mind, the most powerful part of your mind. You can feel and be only the way you want to feel and be. You can achieve success as an athlete which will make you an important part of the team no matter how often you play.

"You can also now suggest to yourself that you will accept only positive thoughts and ideas which are beneficial to you for your well-being and self-improvement as an athlete, in school, and in your personal life. You have the ability to reject all negative thoughts, ideas, suggestions, or inferences from anyone, and you are developing more control over your mind and body.

"Each and every time you encouner a situation where, in the past, you became tense, nervous, upset, or fearful, you will find now that you are more relaxed, calmer, more confident, more sure of yourself. You have the ability to handle situations much better than ever before. You will be able to react better on the playing field, at home, in school, and with your friends.

"Now in a few moments you are going to awaken yourself. You are going to count from zero to five, and when you reach five, you will open your eyes, and you will awaken totally and completely. Physically, you will feel very relaxed. Emotionally you will feel very calm, very peaceful, and very happy. Mentally, you will feel very sharp, very alert, thinking very clearly. And each time you place yourself in the hypnotic state again, you will strengthen your conditioning.

"Zero, 1, 2, slowly and gently you are coming up now. Three, feeling more refreshed, more relaxed, feeling like you have had hours of restful sleep. Four, and *four* becomes a very alert number for you. You begin to feel your breathing changing, the movement in your eyes taking place. Almost awake now. Five. You are wide awake. Say this to yourself: Wide awake. Wide awake."

You have just completed your team's first guided tour into the subconscious mind. This will help them relax and become accustomed to entering the state in which they are most receptive to learning. You should repeat this each practice session for two or three sessions. Then you will want to begin adding suggestions for the team.

Before helping the team through the awakening procedure, add suggestions relating to the learning of plays. These might be to the effect of: "You will be able to concentrate more easily when we discuss the plays. You will have an easier time learning the play books each time you study them. You will find plays becoming a part of your subconscious mind. Each time you study them you will have an easier time learning them. When you hear them called in practice or during a game, your body will respond automatically to where you are to be. You will be able to concentrate on your position, always aware of the other players, playing more naturally and more enjoyably than you have played before. You will be able to use the plays you have learned without having to think about them consciously after they are called." Naturally, you can vary these statements for your team and the sport, but this will give you an idea of suggestions to make.

You can also vary your suggestions to correct team defects. For example, one basketball coach used this technique to help his players learn the different offensive and defensive approaches they would need. Then he discovered that they were all trying to be stars instead of working together. He talked with the team members about this, but the players were too individualistic to continue with the cooperative attitude for very long. Finally, he decided to try the hypnosis technique for improving their playing. He placed them into the state just described, then began making suggestions similar to the following:

"You will constantly be aware of the other team members when you are playing. You will be alert to where they are standing or moving. When there is a chance to score, you will think only of the best way to make that point. You will pass, positioning yourself for a rebound, or take the shot yourself, always choosing the action that will have the greatest chance for success. Your goal will be to make that basket using your teammates to insure there is every chance for success. You will not worry about your personal statistics but about the statistics of the team as a whole."

Obviously, you can use a wide variety of suggestions for all this. What matters is that your suggestions be positive and help the team members overcome team weaknesses. Individual weaknesses can be corrected by the player using this book.

Mastering Personal Conditioning

Knowing the plays is important because the less you have to think about the sport, the better you will play. A number of studies have been made concerning team sports injuries. These studies involved football, baseball, hockey, soccer, and several other games, all of which are generally safe and fun, yet which require techniques and physical action in which there is always some risk of injury. One of the concerns was whether children should begin playing sports early or if they should wait until their bodies are more developed because of the risk of injury.

The first discovery that was made was that team sports should be modified to accomodate changes in growth patterns. For example, suppose you enjoy playing baseball. Perhaps you played baseball from the time you were a small boy or girl. This may have been in one of the Little League–type programs, or it may have been a sandlot pick-up type of game with some friends in the neighborhood. If you did play from the time you were small, you probably remember that certain aspects of the game were easier than others. You could catch, field, and bat easier than you could throw the ball. And if you tried pitching, you often seemed to hurt from what is sometimes known as Little Leaguer's Elbow.

The reason for his is that your body grows in ways which make some actions, which are perfectly harmless for a fully developed male or female, difficult and possibly dangerous for a child. Pitching, for example, should not be done until the bone development is complete, often a year or longer after you reach full height. Yet other skills can be mastered safely from the time you are small.

You might think that football is a game which requires full development because of the body contact. However, because children are both lightweight and proportional to each other in size, this is not a game where there are restrictions (other than having safety equipment) for the young. The passing of the football does not effect the bone structure the way pitching a baseball does, since the movements are very different.

The same situation is true with soccer as it is with football. Soccer is a game which is extremely stressful for the knees. However, when they learn it young, players find that they have a relatively easy time mastering this sport.

What does all this mean for you? The conditioning techniques you will need to master for success in the game are determined, in part, by how early in life you learned the sport you are enjoying. Ideally, you at least will be in high school before you practice pitching in earnest. At the same time, you will have the greatest success with soccer, football, and similar sports if you learned them when a child. However, no matter when you start a sport, a conditioning process coupled with the proper subconscious mind programming can insure that the new player has as much potential for personal success as the individual who has been playing for several years.

Your conditioning should be both personal and relevant to your sport. Football players need speed, strength, and stamina. For them, a combination of weight lifting and running are ideal exercises which can be accomplished on their own. Should you use these, go back to the chapters in this book which provide specific help. Keep in mind that the better you condition yourself in these areas, the greater your potential on the playing field.

For soccer, the conditioning may primarily be running. Remember that I am separating the necessities of conditioning from the techniques of the sports. Most sport require stamina and, in some cases, strength. Certainly the more activities you enjoy which also strengthen your body, such as use of the Nautilus and similar machines, or weight lifting, the better your total physical condition. But it is in cardiovascular activities, such as aerobic conditioning and running, that you will find the greatest value. The problem is that these are not your main interests, and you will have a tendency to do them only when absolutely essential. Yet if you could develop a conditioning program separate from the practice for the sport you love, you would be able to improve your playing ability.

Turn back to the chapters on running and weight lifting. Read these, and consider using them for part of your conditioning process. If you are in school, you should try not only walking to and from school but also taking roundabout routes which enable you to walk a mile or two each way for conditioning. This walk should be relaxed but extremely rapid.

If you work, try parking your car several blocks from your job. Some people also find that it helps to take the steps instead of the elevator or escalator if their offices are on an upper floor. The regular, rapid climbing of a staircase is an excellent conditioning device, even though your job might otherwise be rather sedentary.

You can reinforce this conditioning, admittedly a potentially boring aspect of getting ready for your sport, by using self-hypnosis. After you have relaxed yourself and entered a state of self-hypnosis as discussed in Chapter 3, make suggestions such as the following:

"I enjoy warming up for [name your sport]. I feel better when I take the time to exercise my body each day. When I run [do aerobic exercises, etc.], I feel stronger, more alert, in better control. I know I am becoming a better player for myself and a better member of the team each time I work out to build my cardiovascular system."

Some athletes are extremely limited in the time they can spend doing this type of body-building activity. If you have a set time for running or similar exercises, you might use that time in your mental conditioning. "Each morning, when I go out to run, I feel more awake, alert, better able to start the day. I awaken looking forward to my exercise. If I am unusually tired, I know I will feel better when I am done. If I am alert and anxious to get to work, I know that I will feel even better, more in control, and filled with even greater energy."

If you exercise like this after work or after school, you might say: "When I run, I relax and feel better about myself. Any extreme tiredness seems to be lifted from my shoulders. I feel happy, relieved to be through with the cares of the day. I will be able to better enjoy my evening, be more alert and happy because I have run. If I am tense, my burden will be lightened. If I am depressed, my mood will be buoyed."

Naturally, you can vary what you say. It is important only that your statements be positive, reinforcing what might otherwise seem to be a burdensome choice.

Basic Workouts with the Team

Team workouts are an excellent time to discover your weaknesses, strengths, and the areas of interaction on which you should be concentrating. Are you the type of player who tries to be a star? Are you constantly seeking ways to personally make points, or are you aware of the other players around you and the potential for scoring through interaction, and seeking to work with the others toward the common goal?

Usually there are several possible problems during basic workouts, according to the athletes who have come to see me. The first is "show-boating." You want to prove how good you are so you constantly are trying to personally excel. However, personal excellence in team sports means that you are thinking not of yourself but of the goals of the team.

A second problem is fear and confusion. There are a great many individuals running around the playing field. There is noise, confusion, and people traveling in ways which can make them blurs seen out of the corner of your eye. Even worse, in a sport such as football they may be trying to knock you down, a situation for which the natural reaction is the fight-or-flight syndrome. Under such conditions, fear can develop. This is perfectly normal. It is seldom discussed, but it can affect your performance. The confusion may also cause you to have difficulty concentrating on catching the ball, blocking, scoring a goal, or whatever else you should be doing, depending upon the sport.

A third problem is stamina. The excitement of the playing field can affect your breathing and muscle control. The tension can cause you to tire easily, strain a muscle, or otherwise not be able to go all out for your physical conditioning.

And a fourth problem is the ability to play well under stress. The actions you take need to come automatically. When you have to think extensively about them, you may have periods when you clutch and forget what you are doing. This slows your reaction time.

The counters for these areas are quite simple. First, determine where your problems exist. Then place yourself in a self-hypnotic state and make the following suggestions.

1. To counter trying to excel separately from the need of the team: "When I am on the playing field, my interest is in helping my team score. I will take great pride in every play my teammates accomplish successfully. I will find I am happiest when I work with others to score. I will be uncomfortable trying to make points if the scoring could have been handled more easily by my passing the ball [or shifting the hockey puck, or whatever is appropriate] to someone else." Naturally, with all of these problems, you can vary the suggestions to fit your needs. The important point is that the suggestions all be positive and stress team cooperation over personal glory. If you alter your subconscious so that your pride comes from the team's accomplishments and not just those actions which you take, you will be more successful.

Visualization techniques: Picture yourself in situations where you might be able to push to score, but by involving your teammates you will have the best chance for scoring. For example, you are on the basketball court just far enough from the basket that you might miss the shot. You have the ball, the crowd is cheering, and you want to make a jump shot. You know you have successfully made them in practice from that distance, but you also know you have missed more often than you have made them.

Instantly, you glance all around, suddenly spotting a team member in a better position to try for a basket. You see that you can pass the ball, so you do. Your teammate makes a lay-up that is perfect, and your team scores. You have helped your team achieve two points, and you feel good about yourself.

You also can use other visualization techniques, though they all should be similar. Always, you are in a situation where you can score in whatever sport you are playing. And always there should be another person from your team who is in a little better position. You let the other person make the score, and you feel better about yourself as a result.

2. To counter fear and confusion. For fear, make such suggestions as: "I am a trained athlete in good condition. I have kept myself in at least as good shape as the other players. I understand the game and know that everyone is trying to do his or her best.

"Each time I think about practice, I become relaxed, happy, looking forward to being on the field [the rink, the gymnasium floor, etc.] with my other teammates. When I approach the playing field [or rink, etc.], I become increasingly happy about participating. I am relaxed, in control, my body comfortable with the game to be played and the people who will be running all about (or skating, or whatever).

"Football [soccer, basketball, hockey, etc.] is extremely enjoyable. When I think about the game, even when I am on the field, I will become happy and relaxed. I am confident of my abilities and comfortable with the plays."

Visualization technique: Picture yourself playing in situations where you have been frightened. Start your visualization just before you normally become tense or fearful. Picture yourself relaxing, becoming quite happy as the circumstances on the field change and you are thrown into the confusion which, in the past, has made you uneasy. Then take yourself through the experience, picturing yourself becoming relaxed, happy, able to feel in full control.

If your fear is of being out of control, such as being tackled on the football field, take yourself through that experience. Perhaps you are running with the ball. You see an opposing player coming for you. Instead of being tense, you relax, delighting in the challenge of trying to elude the opponent. You move about, running and dodging, but it is to no avail. You are finally brought down, your body completely relaxing as you feel your opponent's hands touching your body. You fall, roll, and stand unhurt. You may not have wanted to be tackled, but you rise relaxed and happy, knowing it is a part of the game and that you did your best to elude your pursuer. There was no serious problem with what happened, and you know that the next time you may be able to gain even more yardage before you are tackled.

Obviously, you will have to vary this technique for the sport, but when you do, you will find that you are reinforcing the positive verbal suggestions.

Confusion on the field is a little different from fear. With confusion, you are feeling overwhelmed by all the people coming toward you. You need to be able to better focus your attention on the important players surrounding you and on your role with the team. Suggest:

"As I go on the field, I find my concentration narrowing to the role I am to play. I am constantly aware of what I am to do and where I am to go as the action keeps shifting all around me. The other players seem to become an unimportant blur, like the passing of clouds. I remain aware only of those players who matter to me. Wherever I move, I am aware only of the team's goal and those players who can help me achieve that goal."

With a sport such as football, you might add such suggestions as: "When I have the ball, I will be aware of the players trying to tackle me only when they are close enough that I have to plan evasive action. I will carry the ball toward the goal without worrying about everyone else on the field. I will feel comfortable with my speed and maneuvering. I will be relaxed as I run, knowing that my teammates are trying to cover for me. I will feel quite happy as I run through the midst of the confusion, knowing it does not concern me. Only when I am threatened with a tackle will I be alert to those close to me who are trying to stop me, and then I will maneuver around the danger."

Sports such as basketball can have confusion, not only because of the movement on the court but also because of the way the movement of the ball may be blocked. An opponent may be moving in front of you, jumping up and down and waving his or her arms in front of your face. Again, you will modify your suggestions for such circumstances.

"I will relax when I have the ball. The sight of an opponent waving his or her arms and trying to block me will not cause me concern. I will be relaxed, alert to my other teammates and the basket. I will note the movements of my opponent only so I can make my move when he or she is off guard. I will be comfortable passing the ball or bouncing it to another player. I will be comfortable faking. I will recognize that I am in control and this fact frustrates my opponent. I will stay calm, relaxed, able to move in any way necessary in order to score effectively."

The visualization techniques are similar to those used when you experience fear during the game. You simply picture yourself in action, your body calm and relaxed, your movements the ones you would like to make, regardless of the confusion all around which ones would have been unnerving for you.

3. To counter loss of stamina: You have stamina when you go on the playing field. You developed it through the conditioning process discussed earlier in this chapter. The problem you are having comes from nervousness and tension. Thus this is what you will counter.

"I am relaxed as I approach the playing field. I can feel myself breathing easily, comfortably. My body is loose, my muscles relaxed and feeling good. I am pleased with my body, the way I feel, and the excitement of the game.

"As I play, I remain relaxed. My body works automatically. I will run, jump, or do anything else necessary for the game as I play, always relaxed, always happy, my muscles moving smoothly. I am comfortable as I play, breathing smoothly, evenly, always in control."

Visualization techniques: Picture yourself on the playing field (rink, gymnasium, etc.) being relaxed. Take yourself mentally through those circumstances where you once became tired. Picture yourself breathing easily and more relaxed as you play. Picture yourself breathing easily and naturally, even after running and dodging your opponents.

4. To counter stress: Suggest to yourself, "When I play, I feel relaxed, happy, delighted to be on the team. My body feels good. I remember the training I have had. I remember the workouts I've completed. I know that I am a good team player. I know that I am competent to take my part for the team. And this knowledge relaxes me. It makes me happy. I am able to move automatically on the field, easily remembering my role. I am comfortable when others come at me and I must vary my strategy. The greater the tension for scoring, the more I relax, moving naturally, enjoying the game. And the longer we play, the closer the score, the happier I become because of the challenge. I am relaxed, moving naturally, doing my best each time."

Visualization techniques: These are similar to the others. You will picture yourself in the game during periods when you have experienced high stress in the past. You will be relaxed at these times, enjoying yourself, playing effectively. You will move automatically, and if you can remember how your body and muscles felt as you moved down the field, you will recall this in the visualization. You will picture yourself maintaining your confidence and abilities.

Preparing for the Games

Competition brings its own stresses, but most of them are variations of what you experience on the playing field during practice sessions. Thus the techniques you have learned for the practice sessions will apply equally to the games. The only difference is that your suggestions should include the name of the team you are going to face, and your visualization should picture the other players and their uniforms, when possible. If you have no idea what your opponents will be wearing, just use their team name for your suggestions and visualize a general opposition.

If there are certain star players who have dominated the field and limited your actions in past contests, use them in your visualization techniques. This will help you gain confidence against them. However, also visualize other players taking the positions of the stars and playing against you. In this way, your subconscious mind will be programmed for any situation, an important factor if the star is injured or pulled from the game for some reason. The sight of a substitute might otherwise needlessly unnerve you.

The only new problem which can happen in competition but probably will not occur in practice games is pressure due to the sense of the importance of the event. The more you compete, the more you will find that there are few coaches or fans who consider the clash of two teams to be just a game. It may be the "match of the century." It may be "the most intense rivalry any two schools could have." It may be "the battle of titans." It may be "the most important game of the season." Or it may be some other equally intimidating title.

Pressure builds with competition. You feel as though you must act differently than you would otherwise. The time on the playing field is somehow magically transformed into an event of immense historic importance for your school, the community, the state, the nation, or some cosmic force beyond earthly understanding. Even more important, when you hear this type of description, there is a tendency to be pulled into similar emotional state in which you believe all this.

The reality is that you are going to play a game. The fate of the world does not rest on the score. Future generations will not remember who played or how they scored. The monetary madness will dissipate quickly, and what is really just a game will again be just a game.

Knowing the reality and being able to cope with it are not the same. High schools will have pep rallies. You may have to be bused to a game: during the trip the cheerleaders are cheering, everyone may be singing various proschool songs or shouting victory slogans, and the tension builds for you. There may be cheerleaders on the field or on the basketball court. There may be friends, parents, teachers, and others, all rooting for you to win.

Then comes the locker room talk from the coach. A game is suddenly transformed into a spectacular event in which only Superman or Wonder Woman can achieve lasting glory. To lose is to face a crisis of unimaginable proportions. Or so you come to feel before the game starts.

The best time to counter the tension is prior to the game. Sports should be fun. The fate of the universe does not hinge upon how you throw a ball, the final score, or anything else related to sports. Thus you need to plan your suggestions so that your subconscious mind has the game in perspective no matter what outside forces are playing on your emotions.

Place yourself into a state of self-hypnosis, then begin to suggest: "When I play in competition, I feel relaxed and happy. I enjoy the challenge of facing another team. I know that I will play to the best of my ability that day and that I can take pride in that fact. Winning the game is not important to me. Losing the game is not a concern. I will play to the best of my ability and enjoy the game as it unfolds. I will be relaxed, unconcerned about the score. I will work with my teammates to do the best we can and take pride in the results, whatever they may be."

As the game draws closer, you can use similar suggestions, this time naming the team and the specific date of play. You might add some specific suggestions for dealing with the crowd reaction if this is often strong and upsetting for you.

"When we play against _____ [name the opposing team], I will hear the crowd as though their shouting and cheering were like a passing cloud, drifting through my mind. I will not be concerned with what they are saying. I will be pleased that they are feeling the excitement of the game. I will take pride in the fact that I am part of the spectacle that is providing them with entertainment. If they seem angry, I will know it is because they are enjoying the challenge we are facing. But I will always concentrate first on the game. I will recognize that it is enjoyable. I will recognize that I am doing my best as a team player and will take pride in the results, no matter what they may be."

For the Coach

Traditional coaching methods usually involve attempting to "fire up" your players. You want them to care about the competition. If you are a professional coach, chances are that your ability to have your contract renewed and/or the rate of pay which you receive are all determined by your win-loss ratio. Thus you have followed the traditional approaches of using locker room pep talks and trying to stress the importance of each game.

The reality is that high-pressure coaching tactics often can be self-defeating. A skilled coach can truly fire up a team, often turning a losing situation into a winning one. Unfortunately, that same fired-up team may be playing against a superior, equally fired-up team. Under such circumstances, unless your team is extremely lucky, it will lose. Emotions and attitude count for much in winning, but talent, luck, and numerous other factors outside your control can also affect the game.

When a fired-up team loses a game, there can be consequences which were not anticipated. The team members will be discouraged. They may question their abilities and the faith you placed in them. Ideally, this will lead only to brief discouragement followed by a renewed determination to win the next game. But what if this situation does not occur?

You have expressed faith in your players. The fans have expressed faith in them. You have fired their spirits, driving them to play better than ever before, and in their minds they have failed. Even worse, they have failed twice in a row, a fact which is likely to cause them to rethink their abilities. They may begin subconsciously to feel that they cannot win, that their team is limited in ability. This can lead to their holding back on their efforts, not because they wish to do so but because they have subconsciously become losers.

The solution to this problem is to use the modified self-hypnosis technique discussed at the start of this chapter. Have your team relax, and begin making positive suggestions such as:

"When you go against _____ [name the team you will be playing next], you will feel relaxed, in control, trusting in your fellow team members to work together. You are going to get great pleasure from the scoring our team does. You are going to enjoy the offensive plays. You are going to work together to score, taking pride each time one of our team members scores a touchdown [makes a goal, gets a basket, or whatever].

"You are also going to enjoy defensive play. You are going to enjoy keeping the other team from scoring. You are going to have great pleasure in working with your teammates to hinder _____ [name the other team] from making a basket [scoring a touchdown, or whatever].

"The score will not matter to you. You will be relaxed no matter what the score. You will be relaxed no matter what the crowd is shouting. Your pleasure will come from making points. You are going to enjoy working to the best of your ability as a team to make points. No matter how long the game lasts, you are going to feel fresh, relaxed, taking pleasure in making points.

"No matter how hard the other team works, you are going to take pleasure in keeping them from scoring. It does not matter how many points they score. Your pleasure will come from giving _____ [the team] the most difficult time you can, working with your teammates for the best defense possible."

Naturally, you can vary this approach as you desire, though you must remain positive and you must avoid being overly concerned about the scoring.

"Wait a minute!" you are probably shouting. "I was made coach in order to win this game! What do you mean, I shouldn't talk about winning? I'll get fired. I'll be laughed at. I'll be . . ."

Stop! Just a few paragraphs ago I showed you that an emphasis on winning can lead to a psychological reaction which is self-defeating. A couple of losses, and soon the team begins to think of itself as a loser. Your players try, but they are so discouraged they no longer can put out 100 percent. Even worse, if you happen to have a season during which your team is excellent but is playing against even more experienced, highly skilled teams, the players could feel they are worthless even though they are more than a match for most other teams elsewhere. Thus the entire future of some of your players could be shattered.

Now take a closer look at the suggestions I am having you make. I am having you tell the players that they will enjoy playing offense. I am having you suggest that they will make points without worrying about the score. And I am having you take them to a level where they enjoy playing defense, working together to keep the other team from scoring.

What makes for a winning team? They score to the best of their ability, at the same time keeping the other team from making points. The better they do this, the higher the score in their favor. Thus you are convincing them to win, but in a way which does not work against them if they lose.

For example, suppose the worst possible situation arises and your players are up against an equally motivated team which has more experience and greater skill. Your team will, predictably, lose. They may play the sport to the best of their ability. They may play better than they did during some previous game when they were able to destroy the other team. But they are simply outclassed, something which happens to everyone at some time or another.

Now let's make this bad situation even worse. Your players go against two or three such superior teams in a row. Naturally, they lose every game, no matter how good a showing they may make.

Assuming you have used an approach which emphasizes winning, you are likely to have a mighty discouraged team. After all, they may have played better than they ever played before. They may have worked better under pressure, done better interacting with each other, and generally triumphed as a team, despite the loss. But they did lose, not once but repeatedly. And the result can be depression, a desire to give up, to not play to capacity again because everything seems futile.

With the change in subconscious programming I am suggesting, a quite different situation arises. Your players may be slightly discouraged by the losses, but that is not a great concern to them. They take delight in discussing the scoring they made, the ways they prevented the other teams from scoring or at least made it harder for them to win. There is a pride in the way the game is played to the best of their ability, rather than discouragement because they did not win.

The results of this change are that the players concentrate on improving their skills as a team. They work harder at offense. They work harder at defense. They feel positive about their abilities and are anxious to again pit their skills against other teams. The losses no longer matter to them. The triumphs still come, but they come without the risk that the team might not play to full capacity because of discouragement. Thus your motivation actually is stronger, your chance for having a winning team is even greater, and you are achieving what you have desired from the start.

Naturally, you can use other approaches, though it is important that you never stress winning as the goal. You might make suggestions to increase aggressiveness among the players. You might work on rebounding, intercepting passes, stealing the puck, or whatever else is important for the team sport you are coaching. But you always must stress positive actions which can be achieved no matter what the final score. In this way you will have the type of winning team you desire without the risk of creating a counter-program which might lead to failure in the long run.

The handicapped athlete

12

The last time I had the pleasure of watching Jeff bowl, he rolled an average of 180 pins a game. He always had been a semiprofessional bowler, but when he first came to see me, his average score was a third of what I saw that night and he was severely depressed. He had lost the use of his legs in an industrial accident six months earlier, and he felt as though he could never enjoy sports again. The idea that he would bowl close to the best scores he had enjoyed before the accident while sitting in a wheelchair seemed almost miraculous to him. But the achievement was no miracle.

Linda was another of my handicapped patients. She was a natural athlete, tall, lean, taking delight in sports ranging from basketball to volleyball to tennis and golf. She had been out jogging the day the drunk driver veered across his lane and struck her as she ran. Her back was not broken, but she sustained so much spinal damage that she was partially paralyzed for several months. She is beginning to learn to walk again but also must spend many hours in her wheelchair. She, too, was depressed. She, too, wanted to return to the athletic events she loved.

Wheelchair basketball became Linda's sport. By the time she was through with her sessions, she was a skilled player, able to shoot baskets as effectively as many players with full physical skills. Naturally, the sports-modified wheelchair she used was slower than running, her blocking and movement less controlled, but since she was playing against other wheelchair-bound athletes, those limitations affected everyone. What delighted Linda was the fact that she could utilize her basket-shooting skills, something she thought she had lost forever.

The image of the handicapped athlete is often needlessly negative. That is not to say that the handicapped athlete can compete with the top athlete who is not handicapped in the same sport and do as well. The more mobility and flexibility you have, the easier you can master athletics. However, the majority of the handicapped athlete's troubles are in the mind, not the body.

How dare I say such things? you may be asking, irate over the implication that I am ignoring the physical disabilities which you, a friend, or a loved one may be enduring. The answer is simple. Everyone is handicapped in athletics to some degree. A person with very short legs will never have the stride of someone with long legs. A five foot two inch basketball player is always going to be at a disadvantage when playing against someone six feet five inches tall. Yet because there is no physical injury involved with the average athlete's handicap, he or she never sees bodily differences as being a concern. The average athlete learns to play with what God provided, the short basketball player developing quick maneuverability, reflexes for jumping, and a variety of shots. The runner with short legs learns to move those legs faster than he or she might otherwise in order to compensate for the lack of stride. And so it goes for all athletes.

When someone is obviously handicapped, the limitations imposed by the disability become blatant. Every time a handicapped person looks in the mirror, has to sit in a wheelchair instead of standing, cannot see because of blindness, or manifests whatever other problem exists, the difficulty is quite obvious. It is bad enough when this handicap began at birth. It is even worse when the handicap results from military service, an accident, disease, or other problem. You are constantly reinforcing your differences in your own mind.

The reality is that there are many adjustments you can make to allow for your handicap, adjustments which must begin with the subconscious change to positive motivation. Then, when you begin working around your handicap, you will discover far more potential than you ever imagined.

Take Jeff, the wheelchair-bound bowler, as an example. He was a semiprofessional who had mastered the sport before he lost the use of his legs. He would take his rapid steps, his arm moving back, his eye on the pocket he wanted to hit, and bowl strike after strike. He understood how to use his body as it existed to achieve the end he desired.

Suddenly Jeff was in a wheelchair. In his mind he was remembering all the "correct" techniques, trying to do the same movements in a wheelchair that he had used when able to walk. It did not work, and Jeff became frustrated.

In therapy, Jeff came to understand that he would never walk again. He was always going to have the limitations imposed by the wheelchair. He would need to follow the same principles for aiming and rolling the ball he always had, but he would now have to plan a different approach. He could not utilize the momentum of a running start, so he switched to a heavier ball, then shifted the chair so that, from the sitting position, he could use the same spot he had always used to go for the pocket. The shifting of position and the use of a heavier ball to compensate for his inability to add the power of a swing resulted in the gradual return to his old skill. Instead of failing because he could not bowl the way he had in the past, he learned to bowl within his limitations and discovered he was almost as skilled.

Visualization

If you are handicapped and have been reading other sections of this book, you will remember that I frequently suggest that you visualize a skilled athlete in your sport, then mentally place your body on that athlete's. You will then be seeing yourself duplicating what that person has achieved, a powerful reinforcer for your own training.

The problem most suddenly handicapped athletes have is that they are trying to do the same thing they would have done before the injury. They visualize an athlete without a handicap and want to emulate that person. This is physically impossible, and what could have been a powerful tool for positive change suddenly becomes a negative program.

The solution is to visualize a skilled handicapped athlete and use the same techniques as before. In this way, you are imitating someone with the same strengths and limitations you have. What is possible for that person is also possible for you.

Depending upon where you live, you may not have seen someone with your limitations participating in the same sport. When this is the case, you must plan visualization around your handicap instead of bemoaning the loss.

For example, suppose your game is basketball. Typically, you always will be competing against others who are wheelchair-bound so the inability to maneuver quickly is no longer a concern. Both offense and defense will be slowed by their chairs, so your only concerns are rebounding and making baskets.

You already know how to aim for a basket and the different types of shots you can make from a distance. You will no longer be able to slam-dunk the ball or do a lay-up since you can't leap into the air. However, all other shots can be made with simple practice. You are just learning to shoot as though you were suddenly shorter. This means changing your angle to the basket slightly and throwing somewhat harder than you did when standing. It is not at all difficult, just different.

Sometimes you can have an instructor help with modification. There are many handicapped individuals who enjoy karate and the other martial arts. Schools which recognize the abilities of the handicapped will modify the techniques for the wheelchair user. The instructor will often sit in the wheelchair in order to do forms and work out blocks, punches and, when possible, kicks. The normal techniques will be modified to compensate for the arms of the chair and the limited body movements. The person is treated as an equal, the only difference being in the way he or she must work.

A typical example of this situation is a karate expert in the American Tae Kwon Do Association. He lost the use of his right arm to polio, and he has two-thirds of his upper body weight on his left side from the illness, a fact which greatly affects his balance. He learned to shift his balance and use the same arm for both blocks and punches when doing forms or sparring. He is now a top-ranking black belt instructor, able to teach anyone, regardless of whether they are able to use their entire bodies or are handicapped.

Adjusting to What Must Be

With some sports, you are going to have to adjust to the realities of your limitations and accept that you never will play the same type of game you once did. Wheelchair tennis limits your movements. Two handicapped players once may have been cut-throat competitors, always forcing their opponents to run all over the court. Once in wheelchairs, though, they can not maneuver effectively. They have to learn to place the ball closer to the opponent so that little maneuvering is necessary. Otherwise whoever hits the ball first will always win, and there is no enjoyment. A fast-paced player used to running all over the court must settle for a game which is more like volleying for service. This change is forced by the limitations of the wheelchair and cannot be altered.

Likewise the long-distance runner can still enjoy competition when in a wheelchair, but the lower body will no longer be exercised. Now it is the upper body which is developed, hands, arms and shoulders moving the chair along the track or down the road.

The blind must learn to rely upon their hearing and other senses to participate in sports. Someone who is used to watching the pitcher when playing baseball will no longer be able to keep an eye on the ball. Instead, a "talking ball" will generate a tone signal so the blind batter can keep track of where it is. He or she must learn to listen for the approach, swinging the bat when the ball sounds at the right point instead of being able to see it. This is time-consuming and difficult, but no more difficult than when you developed the proper eye-hand coordination for conventional batting when you were a child.

The same is true for blind bowling. You use a pin which generates a tone in order to find your spot. All the other movements are the same, but now your ears do for you what previously had been accomplished only with your eyes.

Some final words

13

There are far more sports than have been covered in this book. This is not because many sports do not fit the approaches discussed. Rather it is because I have tried to touch on a wide variety of activities from which you can adapt the techniques for any other sport you enjoy.

The first step when reviewing a sport not covered specifically in this book is to think of the problems which you might have encountered or those areas of concern. For example, skiers have different problems at different levels of experience. A beginning skier may wish to concentrate on relaxing while in skis. The beginner may want to think about the proper body position and the feeling experienced when standing or moving correctly. Visualization techniques should involve your instructor or a skilled amateur or professional whose movements you have seen and admired. You will program your subconscious so that you are relaxed both on skis and when you have the occasional fall experienced by even professional skiers.

Next a skier might wish to work on specific techniques, such as jumping or the slalom. Always remember that you are using the methods to reinforce your technique and skills. You do not use them to try to be the greatest skier who ever lived or to win a competition. You program your mind to do your best and to handle yourself correctly, factors which will lead to whatever achievements are possible at your present skill level, considering your competition.

Volleyball will bring other concerns. These might be serving, spiking, or any other area which is difficult for you or which you are trying to improve.

Fencing, handball, archery, riflery, and numerous other sports all follow the same techniques. You concentrate on those areas where improvement is desired, combining the positive suggestions with visualization when possible. You use your basic knowledge of the sport and the practice you routinely enjoy as the basis for your suggestions. In this way you will find yourself constantly improving.

Pressures During the Game

The majority of this book has been designed to help you prepare for improved play and the competition you will face. The more you practice the techniques discussed in this book, the more relaxed you will be when you play. Your movements will be automatic. Your actions will be effective no matter what happens with the competition.

When you first use the techniques in this book, the reinforcement will not be so strong as to be certain of getting you through a game. Problems can arise, and you may find that you are uncomfortable when under the stress of competition.

Many athletes who have used self-hypnosis for several years will actually throw themselves into a state of self-hypnosis while playing when they feel pressured. They take advantage of timeouts, half-time breaks, and other lulls in the play to reinforce whatever suggestions are important to them. This is probably not realistic for you, but you can attempt some modified actions which will reduce the stress.

Start by letting yourself relax. You might close your eyes or look away from the distraction of the players and fans. Then begin breathing deeply, slowly, concentrating on calming yourself and ridding your mind of thoughts of the game. Inhale deeply through your nose, exhaling through your mouth. Inhale through your nose, exhale through your mouth. There will be noise all around you, people moving, the crowd cheering, but let the sounds wash over you like a gentle wave lapping at the beach.

Now give yourself positive suggestions such as: "I am relaxed. I am enjoying the game. I feel all the tensions draining from my body." Repeat variations of these suggestions, then relate whatever concerns you might have.

For example, you might say: "As I start to serve the tennis ball, I will feel relaxed, in control, the power building in my body so that my serve is hard and effective." Or "When I start to run down the playing field, I will be alert to the movement of the football. I will be able to catch it, intercept it, or help protect my teammates who are getting the ball." Or you might use whatever else is appropriate for the concerns you are experiencing at the moment.

You will have only a couple of minutes in which to take such action, but a couple of minutes is all you need. You are not reentering the hypnosis process but reinforcing the positive suggestions you previously planted in your subconscious. In this way, you are improving your chances to successfully follow all the programming you developed earlier. Even if you do have some problems, keep in mind that self-hypnosis strengthens the subconscious programming with time. The improvement in your ability will build with repetitions. It is natural to occasionally have some problems, and the relaxation techniques mentioned will help.

Nutrition and the Mind

This book is not meant to include personal health. It is not a "diet and exercise your way to fame in sports" type of book. However, there are a few points which should be mentioned because they are critical factors in your concentration and memory.

Nutrition affects both your mind and your body. When you are under stress, and this can come from the situation on the playing field, your concerns about improving, or even when you are having fun working out, there are nutritional needs which must be met. If you deny your body these needs, you are likely to experience tiredness, an inability to concentrate, and difficulty learning. This situation is magnified if you attempt to use a stimulant to help you on the field.

There are two basic nutritional areas of greatest concern. One is with vitamin C, and the other is with what are known as the B-complex vitamins. These are the vitamins which have the greatest affect on stress and preparing your body and mind for sports.

Vitamin C is often called "the stress vitamin." It is the vitamin we use when we are faced with both positive and negative stress. You use vitamin C if you are a football player running with the ball and you suddenly spot five members of the opposing team surrounding you and about to smash you into the ground. That instant of fear at the moment of recognition leads you to have a loss of vitamin C to try and handle the stress.

At the same time, vitamin C can be lost through positive stress. For example, you are playing football, running down the field with the ball, and suddenly you see that your way is clear to the goal posts. You know the other team members are chasing you, but your lead is so great and your legs moving with such a rapid stride that there is no way they can stop you. You are succeeding. You are going to make the touchdown and win the game. You are happy as you run, elated, letting the cheers of the fans flow over your body. And you are also experiencing what is known as positive stress, again creating a need for vitamin C.

Your ability to react is often determined by choline, one of the B-complex vitamins. Choline affects the nerve synapses, that portion of the body which help the mind control what you do and how quickly you do it. There is a gap between the time you notice a player running toward you and the moment you are able to take evasive action. This gap, a tiny fraction of a second, is made longer when there is nerve synapse damage from poor diet (usually high in sugar and white flour), and it is quickened when you have an adequate supply of choline. Since sweets rob the body of all the b-complex vitamins, including choline, many sports enthusiasts relying upon candy bars and other sweets for "quick energy" will find that they are actually working against themselves. During the course of the game, the rush of adrenalin they felt for the metabolizing of the sugar has led to a sugar deficiency and a B-complex deficiency. You become fatigued and are slower in reacting to the game.

Niacinamide, actually a form of vitamin B-3, and pantothenic acid, also a B-complex vitamin, are natural tranquilizers. Research by the inventor of the pharmaceutical Valium, a drug to which some people have become addicted, indicates that niacinamide can cause the same relaxation response with no risk of addiction or abuse. Niacinamide and all the B-complex vitamins are water soluble. If you take more than you need, you pass the rest in your urine. Thus many athletes, trainers, and doctors working with athletes now suggest the taking of niacinamide and pantothenic acid in combination to serve as a muscle relaxer and calmative. Most important, this combination does not slow you down or make you tired before or during a game. It can help you sleep more comfortably the night before if you are tense, but it will not prevent you from getting "psyched-up" for the competition. It will also not slow your reaction time in any way.

Vitamin B-6 is sometimes called "the memory vitamin" because it helps the mind relax and vent problems in your sleep. People who are having trouble dreaming and remembering will take vitamin B-6 in order to have more dreams. This can be extremely relaxing and helps you prepare for your game.

In addition to all the mental exercises you have learned, it will help for you to learn more about nutrition. You should consult a nutritionist or a doctor with nutrition training for specific recommendations. However, as a general rule, you will find that adults engaged in athletics often will benefit by taking a good multiple vitamin and multiple mineral tablet every day. Do not go by brand, but read the ingredients on the different labels and compare what you are actually getting. You should not buy a vitamin that contains sugar, and many do, nor should you assume that a vitamin is "best" because it is advertised. Also, the MDR, or Minimum Daily Requirement, is not a good estimate of what you need. It is not based on research, and many traditional thoughts about minimum needs are being rejected by researchers today. Usually you need far greater quantities of vitamins than just those called for by the MDR.

Most athletes will want to take at least one gram and often as much as 3 grams (3000 milligrams) of vitamin C spread throughout the day. This vitamin also helps with healing of injuries.

Taking a vitamin B-complex 100 supplement is a wise idea; often taking two or three spread throughout the day is best. Vitamin B-complex 100 offers one hundred milligrams or one hundred micrograms of each B vitamin. You can also use the vitamin B-complex 50 or vitamin B-complex 125 tablets, depending upon what is available in your area. What is important is that you always take those tablets which contain an equal quantity of each vitamin. Tablets marked "Super B complex" or some other terms have varying amounts of each vitamin because some are cheaper to synthesize than others. However, it has been found that when you take a B-complex tablet, you will not gain full benefit without taking equal quantities of each. It is only with supplemental B vitamins, such as niacinamide and pantothenic acid, taken singly, that you can vary the amounts and have the nutritional quality be effective.

Vitamin B-12 is a natural stimulant for those who have trouble getting up in the morning. Researchers have found that men and women who claim they cannot get started without the stimulation of a cup of coffee in the morning actually have a vitamin B-12 need. There is no need for caffeine or any artificial stimulant, all of which can affect your performance as an athlete. Instead, the taking of 2000 micrograms of B-12 in time release form provides the type of full release of energy often desired.

As I mentioned, your specific needs should be determined by a nutritionist. However, as a general rule the following dietary suggestion will enable you to maintain an effective mental and physical condition for achieving your best as an athlete.

Juices: Many athletes feel that they must drink Gatorade® or some similar electrolyte replacement beverage. This may be of help during periods of high fluid loss but, in general, you are going to need fruit juices or vegetable juices for proper nutrition. These juices should be unsweetened. You may find that orange juice provides the same energy boost you were expecting from a Gatorade or similar beverage during the early stage of thirst. It is also better for you as a regular drink.

Meat: Many athletes think they must have massive steaks in order to build their bodies and prepare for a game. Some football teams routinely dine on steak before a big game, then find the food so difficult to digest when they are under the stress of playing that they become sick to their stomachs.

As a general rule, you will find that meats in general, and especially the organ meats, are all good for you. You can gain the most energy from taking eggs, salmon, liver, organ meats, and even oysters, since these are rich in vitamin B-12. Having liver before a game may be more effective in providing energy for play than having a steak.

Your regular diet should stress fish and poultry over beef because these foods generally have been found to be healthier for you. Over time, beef can increase your cholesterol build-up, among other problems, if you are not careful. Since fish and poultry can be just as effective for your body with less risk down the road, they are recommended.

Fruit: Fresh fruits are excellent for you. If you have any doubts about what they can do for you in maintaining both an electrolyte balance and quenching your thirst, take a look at extreme long-distance runners. They are constantly eating oranges in order to maintain their energy level while running marathon lengths.

Avoid using sugar with your fruit. Ideally, the fruit should be eaten raw, though cooked fruit is also good for you. If you buy canned fruit, see if it is marked water-pack or syrup-pack. Fruit packed in syrup will have sugar.

Always keep in mind that the idea that sugar is an energy food is a partial myth. You will receive a jolt of energy while the sugar is in your body, before the adrenalin is released to metabolize it. Since raw sugar misleads the body into thinking you have eaten a full meal, too much adrenalin is released, the sugar is used, and you suddenly become extremely tired. It is more difficult to participate. It is more difficult to think clearly. You become tired, rather depressed, and may have difficulty responding to your subconscious programming as well as to your conscious desires to excel. What seemed like a quick lift can work against you by the end of a long game. Thus sugar in any form is best avoided when trying to use nutrition to enhance your mental improvement and physical conditioning.

Vegetables: Fresh, lightly cooked, canned (water-pack only), and frozen (no sugar added) vegetables are all good for you. Among the most nutritionally sound are such vegetables as string beans, broccoli, tomatoes, cauliflower, avocado, sauerkraut, radishes, asparagus, Brussel sprouts, zucchini, squash, carrots, cabbage, eggplant, green beans, celery, beets, turnips, lima beans, and lettuce.

Many training tables offer not only steak but French fries. The latter have a number of problems when you are eating with the desire to have the nutrition boost your mental conditioning. First, French fries are generally made from skinned potatoes. Yet it is the skin of the potatoes which holds the bulk of the Vitamin C.

Frying the potatoes results in potential problems from the grease. Often deep-fat frying can make the potatoes more difficult to digest. In addition, the fat can be starting to go rancid, a fact which affects you nutritionally even though it may not be noticeable to your taste.

In addition to everything else, most people feel that the only proper way to eat French fries is with them smothered in catsup. Catsup is high in sugar and salt. The sugar will affect your energy level, possibly causing you to tire early, and the salt can affect your blood pressure.

A baked potato is nutritionally excellent and will provide the full food value you need for athletic excellence. It is the preferred form of potato for athletes.

Brown rice is also a good food to eat with your balanced diet. Contrary to the name, brown rice is not "brown" in color. It is slightly darker than processed rice, a fact noticeable only when they are side by side. At the same time, it supplies needed nutrition, something processed rice lacks.

Planning your meals around whole, natural foods will help your athletic performance and reinforce the positive work achieved through self-hypnosis. You will also find that you are more alert, better able to learn, and better able to perform at your best when dietary awareness matches your efforts to mental and physical conditioning.

No matter what your current skill levels, you are a successful athlete right now. You have experienced the joy of the game and the excitement of competition, and have the desire to be the best of which you are capable, even as you are growing in your skills and ability. You have the attitude of a winner, and the fact that you have purchased this book only strengthens my belief in you. You bought it to do better, be better, to reach beyond what you thought might be your best.

By following the program in this book, you have been able to erase the final barrier to achieving top performance—your subconscious negative programming. Reread the sections which relate to your sports interests whenever you are feeling discouraged or having a problem. Practice the self-hypnotic techniques you have learned, and combine them with your regular workouts and competition. You will find that the changes in your ability will be startling. You will be the psychological equal of the top professional athletes, and with this fact as your base, your future potential is unlimited.

Index

Improve Your Sex Life Through Self-Hypnosis

Improve your existing sex life, correct frustrating sexual problems and learn to apply the latest self-hypnosis techniques to this most intimate facet of interpersonal relations. This book clearly defines sexuality - yours and your partner's - to help you improve the quality of personal relationships.
$6.95 each

Self-Hypnosis: The Key to Athletic Success

Whether you are a Professional striving to reach your fullest potential or a weekend athlete interested in improving your performance, learn the most effective hypnotic techniques. Develop the same confidence and motivation that enable top professionals to reach their peak performance.
$6.95 each

AUDIO CASSETTE TAPES

Facing Today and the Future Through Self-Hypnosis

Side 1: Learn your own personalized formula to reach the most effective depth of self-hypnosis.
Side 2: Practice with an easy-to-follow conditioning exercise, which is all you need to learn to tap the endless resources of your subjective mind with this totally new approach to self-hypnosis.
$9.95 per cassette

VIDEO CORRESPONDENCE COURSES

The Professional Hypnotism Training Program

At last, a quality home study program on videotape. You will receive 12 hours (2 video cassettes) of educational video, a textbook, "The Professional Hypnotism Manual", by Dr. John Kappas, and a Student Handbook which contains the necessary educational materials for active learning. This course affords you the opportunity to learn and experience the finest professional hypnosis training available today. Whether you are a beginner learning a new skill, or a professional perfecting your existing techniques, this course will meet your needs.
(VHS only)
$430 per course

Handwriting Analysis

A new and exciting course for professional use or just for fun. You will receive 12 hours (2 video cassettes) of educational video, a textbook, "Grapho-Therapeutics", and a Student Workbook that contains exercises for active learning. Within the Student Workbook are plenty of samples to illustrate this exciting science. Now you can learn Handwriting Analysis in the comfort of your own home, as well as increase your income providing expert professional services such as: Personality Profiles, Personnel Selection, Vocational Guidance, Executive Criteria, Compatibility Evaluation, Diagnostic Evaluation, and Authenticity Verification. Define compatibility with your mate, your family, friends and co-workers, and realize career potentials faster and with greater accuracy than possible before now. (VHS only)

$350 per course

PANORAMA PUBLISHING COMPANY
18607 Ventura Blvd., Suite 310
Tarzana, Ca 91356
(818) 344-4464 or (213) 873-6979
OUTSIDE CALIFORNIA, CALL TOLL FREE 1-800-634-5620

ORDER BY PHONE WITH VISA OR MASTERCARD:

Or simply turn the page and order by mail. Just fill out the form and mail it to the address above. Be sure to include your check, money order, or credit card authorization. Please add the correct shipping charges according to the instructions below.

SHIPPING CHARGES:

BOOKS, AUDIO CASSETTES, AND THE MENTAL BANK REVIEW
Continental U.S.-$3.50 for first item; $.50 for each additional item.

VIDEO CORRESPONDENCE COURSES
Continental U.S. - $7.50 for first item; $3.00 for each additional item.

Please call for information on shipping rates outside the continental U.S.

For a FREE catalog on other material available from Panorama Publishing Co. call (818)344-4464 or outside California (800) 634-5620.

Prices are subject to change without notice.
All orders are shipped via UPS. Please allow 2-4 weeks for delivery
(or if you wish faster delivery, call for information and rates).

ORDER FORM

QTY	TITLE	UNIT PRICE	TOTAL
	Sub-total		
CALIFORNIA RESIDENTS ADD 8.25% SALES TAX			
SHIPPING: See Previous Page			
TOTAL ENCLOSED			

Sorry – No. C.O.D.

Make checks payable to *Panorama Publishing Company*

OR

Use your credit card.

Mastercard # _____

Visa # _____

Expiration Date_____

Signature_____

Name _____

Address _____

City_____

State _____

☐ PLEASE PLACE ME ON MAILING LIST FOR OTHER PUBLICATIONS

ORDER FORM

QTY	TITLE	UNIT PRICE	TOTAL
	Sub-total		
CALIFORNIA RESIDENTS ADD 8.25% SALES TAX			
	SHIPPING: See Previous Page		
	TOTAL ENCLOSED		

Sorry – No. C.O.D.
Make checks payable to *Panorama Publishing Company*

OR

Use your credit card.

Mastercard # _____

Visa # _____

Expiration Date_____

Signature_____

Name _____

Address _____

City _____

State _____

☐ PLEASE PLACE ME ON MAILING LIST FOR OTHER PUBLICATIONS